Jambalaya, Crawfish Pie, filé Gumbo

Cajun and Creole Cuisine

Todd-Michael St. Pierre

Beau Bayou Publishing Company
P.O. Box 53089
Lafayette, Louisiana 70505

Jambalaya, Crawfish Pie, Filé Gumbo

Beau Bayou Publishing Company
Lafayette, Louisiana

For information address:
Beau Bayou Publishing Company
P.O. Box 53089
Lafayette, Louisiana 70505
(337) 769- 1272

ISBN: 1-931600-33-3

Printed in the United States of America

This collection is dedicated to my LeBlanc & Thibodeaux ancestry.

Also to my faithful readers in Quebec, Belgium & France. Merci!

Contents

Foreword

Cajun food is some of the best food on the planet (And not just because I am partial) A typical South Louisiana Kitchen is filled with such ingredients as green onions, celery, parsley, bell pepper, garlic, black & white pepper, ground red pepper and Filé (pronounced fee-lay) which is made from sassafras leaves. Of course a bottle of Tabasco is essential. (See Tabasco.com)

I was born in New Orleans and grew up between New Orleans & Baton Rouge along the Mississippi River. My Grandmother (MawMaw) and my Grandfather (PawPaw) were wonderful cooks. Cajun/Creole cuisine was commonplace in my childhood home. My MawMaw was known for her Gumbo. (In fact, I have yet to taste a better Gumbo than hers) My PawPaw was quite famous for his Jambalaya. (It is safe to say he will always be the Jambalaya King in my book).

I grew up in a family of great cooks and great storytellers. Yes, we were proud of our Cajun (short for Acadian) Heritage. The Cajuns left Nova Scotia in 1755, deported because they refused to abandon their Catholic faith and swear allegiance to England. I write about this in my forthcoming Children's Picture Book "Acadie, I Remember 1755 (How Cajuns came to be) A vast number of the displaced Acadians made their way to South Louisiana.

It is true that most Cajuns and Creoles are more proud of being from south Louisiana than they are of being southerners. Our predominantly French and catholic citizens don't relate so easily to barbecue, rebel pride, or drinking tea with meals. In fact bland and un-seasoned food is often referred to as Baptist food. We strive to preserve our heritage and pass our food and musical traditions along to each new generation and we realize that we are a minority, which tends to make us more tolerant of other minorities. Many of us also wish that our public schools here would teach French, as a required second language, starting in kindergarten. The rest of the South is quite content with its English only, White-Anglo-Saxon-Protestant traditions. We are not cut from that same cloth. Most of my people will attest to the fact that they feel like a fish out of water when visiting other states in the South and all will agree that north Louisiana should definitely be given to Arkansas or Mississippi.

The poems included throughout this collection depict the humor and history of our unique little corner of the world. And theses recipes are for all of you out there who love good New Orleans Creole Cuisine but also enjoy down home Coonass Cooking, too!

Preface

My intention in this book is to present some traditional Cajun and Creole recipes and a few newer but still True-To-Louisiana recipes as well. You'll find all time favorites right along side many innovative town and country dishes.

I want to break from the usual format of most cookbooks by starting with my personal favorite MAIN dishes. (Yes, the way we make Gumbo around here it is definitely a MAIN dish!)

Since I know you're ready for all the good things you either heard about or tasted while on vacation in Louisiana, let's cut through the chase and get right to the "I'd trade your mama for another bowl of that stuff!"

When you're in a hurry, it's always better to have the most popular dishes in the front of the book. This will save you both time and frustration. Of course we must start with Gumbo; The single most popular Cajun dish ever!

These are the recipes that I love and I hope you and yours will enjoy for years to come.

Bon appetit'! Todd-Michael

Raised on Gumbo

Mumbo-jumbo, raised on gumbo,
Fresh pralines for dessert.
Crawfish, claw-fish, please, no raw fish,
Some Coush Coush sure won't hurt.

Growing up Cajun,
If you want a snack…
blackberries growing
In the field out back.

Growing up Cajun,
If you want a treat…
Stuffed Mirliton
Is hard to beat.

Growing up Cajun,
You take it from me…
You know about roux
And fricassee.

That price is nice for Dirty-Rice,
Sugarcane hits the spot.
Mumbo-jumbo, raised on gumbo,
Tabasco's not that hot!

Beaucoup Sherry Gumbo
(pronounced boo-coo)

1cup oil
2 pounds boned chicken meat (Without skin), cut into bite-sized pieces
1 1/2 pounds andouille sausage (or sausage of your choice) cut into bite-sized pieces
1 cup flour
4 cups chopped onion (purple or white)
2 cups chopped celery
2 cups chopped bell pepper
1 tablespoon chopped garlic
8 cups chicken stock (water & bouillon)
salt to your own liking
Tabasco to taste
1 cup chopped onion (green)
1 cup chopped parsley
filé
cooked rice
4 tablespoons Sherry

Sprinkle chicken with drops of Tabasco, Brown in oil over medium heat in Dutch oven.
Add sausage and sauté with chicken. Remove both from pot. Remove from heat and strain fat. To make roux, over low heat, add flour to hot fat gradually, stirring with a whisk. Over low heat, brown the roux, stirring constantly.

Gradually add the stock; mix well. Add the chicken and sausage and bring to a boil.

Reduce to a simmer and cook for an hour or more. Season to taste. 10 minutes before serving, add green onions, parsley and sherry. Gumbo may or may not be served over rice. Add 1/2 teaspoon of filé per serving.

Enough for 10-15 servings.

Aunt Marie's Seafood Gumbo

1/2 or more filet of catfish, redfish or trout
2 pounds Shrimp, peeled and deveined
2 cups chopped onion (Sweet Vidalia if possible)
Gumbo filé
1 gallon water
salt, black and red pepper to taste (Come on put some hair on your chest)
1/2 pint of shelled oysters with liquid
1 cup chopped celery
1/2 teaspoon finely chopped parsley
4 cloves minced garlic

First make your roux (Just as we went over in the last recipe). Add onions and celery to roux. Cook until onions are wilted and then add water and garlic. Cook in heavy uncovered pot over medium heat for one hour. Season to taste with salt, black and red pepper. Add shrimp, parsley and fish to mixture; cook another 15 minutes. Next add your oysters to the mix, let it come to a boil. Serve with cooked rice. Sprinkle with a little filé and Tabasco if you please.

Serves 6.

C'est bien (say byenh)- it's good!

Theriot Family Gumbo
(Pronounced Terry-O)

4 tablespoons oil
4 tablespoons flour
1 medium onion, chopped
1/2 cup chopped celery
1/2 cup chopped bell pepper
3 or 4 slices bacon
1/2 cup ham chunks
3 cloves garlic, crushed
1 pound okra cut in 1/2 inch slices
32 ounces canned stewed tomatoes
1 cup crab meat
2 dozen large peeled shrimp
hot water
salt to taste
2 bay leaves
sprinkle of thyme
sprinkle of black pepper
1/2 teaspoon Tabasco

Take a large pot and heat 5 tablespoons of oil in it. Once well heated, sprinkle and stir 5 level tablespoons of flour. Cook, stirring constantly, until browned but not burnt. Add the onion, celery, bell pepper, and parsley. Simmer for 12 minutes, stirring often.

Chop bacon and add to pot with the ham chunks. Cook another five minutes. Add the garlic and okra. Simmer until okra is no longer stringy, about 15 minutes. Increase heat to high and add tomatoes. Add crabmeat and shrimp.

Pour in enough water to cover the entire mixture, and 1/2 teaspoon salt. Simmer 15 more minutes with the cover on. Add more salt to taste. Add bay leaves, thyme, and black pepper. Cook 20 minutes more and add more water if the gumbo is too thick. (Remember that Gumbo is more like soup than stew) Serve with rice.

Serves 8

(Before you know it you'll say… "C'est parti" (say pahr-TEE) - it's all gone)

Vermillion Gumbo

1 stick butter
2 tablespoons flour
1-pound okra
1 can chicken broth
1 small can V8 juice
24 ounces of water
1 large can boneless chicken
½ teaspoon Cajun seasoning
3 tablespoons dried/chopped onions
1 teaspoon minced garlic
1 (6-ounce) container of crabmeat
1 (6-ounce) container of shrimp
1 (6-ounce) container of clams or oysters
1 teaspoon of filé
1/2 teaspoon Tabasco

In large pot, brown butter and flour lightly on medium heat. Stir in remaining ingredients except seafood and filé. Bring to a boil, lower heat and simmer 30 minutes.

Add seafood with all juices and filé. Now stir and simmer for another 15 minutes. Serve over rice in a bowl.

Serves 6.

Although rather unusual, Vermillion Gumbo is a French Quarter favorite!

Margurite's Green Gumbo

10 ounces Fresh spinach OR 10 ounce package frozen leaf spinach
10 ounces Fresh mustard greens OR 10 ounce package frozen mustard greens
10 ounces Fresh turnip greens OR 10 ounce package frozen turnip greens
10 ounces Fresh collard greens OR 10 ounce package frozen collard greens
1/2 Medium cabbage, shredded
2 Bay leaves, minced
1 teaspoon dried leaf basil
1 teaspoon dried leaf thyme
1 teaspoon dried leaf oregano
1/4-teaspoon ground allspice
1/8-teaspoon Ground cloves
1/4 teaspoon Fresh grated nutmeg
4 qt chicken stock
1 pound Lean boneless pork
1 pound Smoked ham
2/3-cup vegetable oil
2 Large onions, chopped
4 Celery stalks, chopped
1 Large green bell pepper, chop
4 Large garlic cloves, chopped
2 tablespoons sugar
Salt
Fresh ground black pepper
Cayenne pepper
24 Shucked oysters with liquor*

12 Green onions, thinly sliced
1/2 cup Flat-leaf parsley, minced
4 cups hot cooked rice

Tear greens into small pieces. Remove large stalks and ribs. Place cleaned or thawed greens, cabbage, bay leaves, basil, thyme, oregano, allspice, cloves, and nutmeg into a large pot. Add stock and enough water to cover greens. Bring to a boil. Reduce heat. Cover; simmer while preparing remaining ingredients.

Prepare seasoning mix. To prepare Seasoning Mix place all ingredients in a large plastic bag and shake to combine.

Cut pork and ham into bite-size pieces. Add meats to Seasoning Mix. Shake to coat lightly. Set seasoned meat aside while oil heats. Heat oil in a large, heavy skillet over medium-high heat. When oil is very hot, add seasoned meat; stir until brown on all sides. Remove browned meat; add to simmering greens. Reduce heat to medium; add onions, celery, bell pepper, and garlic to skillet. Cook until vegetables are wilted, about 5 minutes.

Remove vegetables with a slotted spoon; add to simmering greens. Stir in sugar; simmer, uncovered for one hour. Season to taste with salt, black pepper and cayenne. Cover; simmer 2 hours.

About 10 minutes before serving, stir in oysters with their liquor, green onions, and parsley. Cook until edges of oysters curl. Serve over rice with filé powder to taste.

Serves 8

Margurite tells me that "Green Gumbo" was Gospel Great and New Orleans native "Mahalia Jackson's" Favorite!

Etienne's Simple & Savory Shrimp Gumbo

3 to 5 pound ready-peeled shrimp
1 pound okra
1 large or 2 small (Preferably red or purple) onions
2 fresh tomatoes
1 tablespoon Shortening
1 red, yellow or green bell pepper)
1 tablespoon Tabasco
1 clove of garlic diced
2 teaspoons vinegar (take my word on this one)
1/4 cup regular sugar
1 teaspoon Creole seasoning

Finely chop okra. Mince Onion. Fry okra onion and bell pepper slightly in shortening.
Add chopped tomatoes. Fry for 2 more minutes. Then add two quarts of boiling water.

Add shrimp, Tabasco, garlic, vinegar, sugar and Creole seasoning to mixture. Boil for about 1 hour and simmer for additional hour. Served with steamed rice.

(Pretty Simple huh?)

Baton Rouge (Cabernet Sauvignon) Gumbo

3 tablespoons vegetable oil
2 pounds round steak cut in small cubes
1/2 pound cubed ham
20 ounces of fresh/cut okra
2 teaspoons Cajun seasoning
3 quarts water
1 beef bouillon cube
1 cup Cabernet Sauvignon wine
1 teaspoon Tabasco
2 tablespoons flour
2 onions finely chopped
1 yellow bell pepper, finely chopped
1 tablespoon minced garlic

Brown meat in oil in large pot. Add ham and stir. Cook for 7 minutes. Remove meat and cook okra in drippings, stirring occasionally till it loses its stringiness. Return meat to pot and season.

Stir in 1 cup of boiling water in which bouillon has been dissolved. Add Tabasco, wine and remaining water and bring it all to a boil. Lower heat, cover and simmer for 70 minutes.

Make your roux with flour and oil stirring over medium heat until browned. Add the chopped onions, bell pepper, and garlic stirring until soft. Stir in one-cup hot water and add your roux to meat pot. Simmer covered for 1 hour. Serve over rice.

Serves 8-10

Be sure and sample the wine as you cook, just don't get too drunk to enjoy your Gumbo!

Ya Gotta Know

If you really wanna trya
To make da Jambalaya,
You gonna need green onion,
So don'tcha use papaya!

When da onion make you crya,
You stir the Jambalaya.
You gonna need some chicken,
Please, don'tcha ask me whya.

You haffta have good sausage,
And no one can denya,
You betta know your spices,
If you cooka Jambalaya.

You slice, you dice, you brown da rice,
Soon kinfolk will replya...
"What all you got in dat dare pot
Dis here's GOOD Jambalaya!"

Some words in the above poem are deliberately misspelled
for phonetic/humorous effect.

Joie de Vivre (Joy of Life) Jambalaya

1/4-cup corn oil
1 pound boned chicken, cut bite-size
1-tablespoon margarine
1 large onion chopped
1/2 green bell pepper, chopped
3 stalks celery, chopped
3 cloves garlic, chopped
1/3-cup water
2 cups canned tomatoes in juice, chopped
1/2 small can tomatoes in juice, chopped
1/2 small can tomato paste
1 fairly decent size piece of tasso (or pork sausage) diced
1/4-teaspoon salt
1/8-teaspoon black pepper
1/2 teaspoon Tabasco
2-1/2 cups cooked white rice

Heat oil in large pot. Add chicken; stir and cook for 10 minutes; remove. Add margarine to pot and stir and cook raw vegetables until wilted. Add water, tomatoes, and tomato paste.
Stir well. Return chicken to pot. Stir in seasonings and tasso. Bring to a boil. Reduce heat; cover and simmer for 40 minutes.

When cooked, add rice. Toss and heat thoroughly. Serve with green salad and bread.

Serves 4-6

If you don't feel Joy after a plate of this get your head examined!

Broussard's Crawfish Jambalaya

1 tablespoon Flour
2 tablespoons Oil, canola preferably
1 cup chopped onions
5 cloves garlic, minced
1 pound Crawfish tails or shrimp
1 1/8 cups uncooked, long-grain rice
1/2 cup chopped celery
1/2 cup chopped green pepper
2 1/2 teaspoons Salt
1 teaspoon Black pepper
1/2 teaspoon Cayenne pepper, or to taste
1 teaspoon Tabasco

In a large pot over medium-low heat, make a roux with flour and oil. Cook stirring constantly, until golden brown and smooth, at least 20 minutes, preferably longer. Add onions and garlic and cook until almost soft. Add 1-1/2 cups cold water and simmer 30 minutes.
Add crawfish and cook about 10 minutes. (Note: if using chicken or sausage, cook ingredients longer to ensure they'll be done when rice is done.) Add 2 more cups of water and bring to a boil. Add remaining ingredients; stir to blend but not too much. Reduce heat to low, cover pot, and cook about 30 minutes or until rice is cooked. Try not to open lid during final cooking. Fluff rice thoroughly with fork before serving.

Serves 4

Yankees, Midwesterners and other non-Cajuns may prefer less pepper. Adjust accordingly!

Anatole's Pork JUMBO laya

3 to 4 pounds pork (cut in cubes)
2 pounds sliced andouille or smoked sausage
1/4-cup oil or bacon drippings
2 cups chopped onion
2 cups chopped celery
1 cup chopped bell pepper (green)
1/2 cup diced garlic
8 cups chicken stock or water
2 cups sliced mushrooms
1 cup sliced green onions
1/2 cup chopped parsley
Salt and cayenne pepper to taste
Tabasco to taste
1/4-cup sugar (Trust me on this one)
5 cups of long grain rice

In a large Dutch oven (preferably cast iron) heat oil or bacon drippings over medium-high heat. Sauté' pork until some pieces are sticking to the bottom of the pot, about 20 minutes. Add sausage and stir an additional 10 to 15 minutes. Drain oil from pot. Add onions, celery, bell pepper and garlic And sugar. Continue cooking until onions begin to become transparent.

Bring to a rolling boil and then immediately reduce heat to simmer. Cook for 15 minutes. Add green onions and parsley. Now add your pepper and salt to taste. Then add the rice, reduce heat to very low, cover and cook thirty to forty-five minutes.
Keep covered.

Serves 10 to 12

(Anatole say's this recipe might not be the healthiest, but it sure is the best tasting!)

Boo's EZ Sausage Jambalaya
(Microwave)

1 tablespoon oil
1/2 cup chopped onion
1/2 cup chopped green onion
1/4 cup chopped bell pepper
2 cups water
2 chicken bouillon cubes
1/2 teaspoon parsley flakes
1/2 teaspoon salt
1/2 teaspoon Tabasco sauce
1 teaspoon Worcestershire sauce
Dash of garlic powder
Pepper to taste
1 cup long grain rice
3 Cajun smoked sausage

In a 3-quart dish, place oil and onion. Microwave on high for 4 minutes. Add remaining ingredients, except rice and meat. Stir and cover. Microwave at 50% power for 12 additional minutes, covered. Let stand 8 to 10 minutes.

Serves 6.

(Easy & quick but tasty too!)

Napoleonville Jambalaya

2 Tablespoons vegetable Oil
2 Large Onions — chopped
1 Green Pepper — chopped
1/2 Cups Chopped Fresh Parsley
3 Garlic Cloves — chopped
2 Pounds Smoked Hot Sausage — sautéed and sliced
1 pound salt pork, boiled 15 minutes — cut into small piece
1 pound black-eyed peas, boiled until about half cooked
6 cups chicken broth
3 cups rice
Salt and freshly ground pepper
1 Bunch green onions — chopped

Heat oil in Dutch oven or other large pot over medium heat. Add onion, green pepper, parsley and garlic, and sauté about 10 minutes. Add sausage, salt pork, peas and chicken broth and bring to boil. Add rice and return to boil. Cover tightly and simmer about 45 minutes; DO NOT LIFT LID.

Season with salt and pepper to taste and add green onion, mixing well. Let stand about 5-10 minutes before serving.

Makes 12 - 16 servings.

A delicious crowd-pleaser!

Sassy Shrimp Jambalaya
(A la Creole)

3 tablespoons oil (or butter)
1 medium onion, chopped
1/2 cup red bell pepper
3/4 cup chopped celery
2 cloves garlic, chopped
1 16-ounce can stewed tomatoes
3/4-cup tomato paste
Salt to taste
1 teaspoon Tabasco
1 1/2 cups boiled shrimp, deveined
1 1/2 cups ham, cubed
1/2 cup chopped green onion tops
2 cups white rice

Heat oil in large heavy saucepan. Stir and cook onion, bell pepper, celery, and garlic until wilted. Add tomatoes and tomato paste. Season to taste with salt, black pepper, and ground red pepper; stir well. Cover and bring to a boil. Reduce heat; simmer for 20 minutes.

Add shrimp, ham, green onion tops, and rice. Toss mixture over low heat until hot.

Serve with a side dish of boiled okra sprinkled with vinegar and/or a green salad.

Serves 4-6.

Crawfish Pie

Hebert's in the backyard with nutria in a sack,
Margurite is making beignets and coffee pitch black.
Pierre plays the accordion, Oh me, Oh my,
I counted four and twenty crawfish baked in a pie.

Twenty-four delicious spicy baked crawfishes,
Nanan's secret recipe served on nice blue dishes.
They're the best in Acadiana, y'all that's no lie,
How'd she fit so many mudbugs in just one pie?

Hebert's in the backyard with oysters in a sack,
Margurite is making beignets and coffee pitch black.
Pierre plays the accordion, Oh me, Oh my,
I counted four and twenty crawfish baked in a pie.

That's Louisiana crawfish, not Chinese we buy,
To get the twenty-four crawfish, for the Crawfish Pie!

(Hebert: Pronounced A-Bear)

Gautreaux's Crawfish Pie

Pie dough enough for 4 individual pies (or two large)
1-1/2 cups crawfish tails; crawfish fat and water to make 2 cups
3 tablespoons cooking oil
2 tablespoons butter
Salt and red pepper to taste
Pinch of thyme
Pinch of nutmeg
4 tablespoons cornstarch
1 medium onion
1/4 cup chopped celery
1 clove garlic, mashed
1/3 cup tomato sauce mixed with 1/3 cup water
1 tablespoon green onion
1-tablespoon parsley

Cook onion, celery and garlic in cooking oil, stirring until tender. Dish out half the cooked mixture. To the mixture add tomato sauce, water and crawfish fat. Cook over medium heat and when it boils, slowly add cornstarch and water stirring until sauce thickens, season with nutmeg, thyme, red pepper and salt to taste.

To the remaining cooked onion mixture in saucepan add crawfish tails, butter, and cook 2 to 3 minutes. Combine sauce, crawfish, green onion and parsley. Cook, then pour into pastry lined pie plates, equally divided. Wet edges of under-crust, cover with upper crust. Press edges together, prick with fork. Bake in a 450 degree preheated oven for 5 minutes. Next reduce heat to 400 degrees and bake about 15 minutes.

(A sweet lady by the name of Isabelle Gautreaux taught me to make Crawfish Pie and I will forever be grateful!) Gautreaux pronounced "Go-trow"

Crawfish Cheese Pie By Celeste Babineaux
(Babineaux pronounced "Ba-bin-no")

1 stick butter
5 stalks celery, finely chopped
1 can cream of shrimp soup (do not dilute)
1/4 teaspoon each; red, black and white pepper
1 pound crawfish tails
1 cooked piecrust
5 ounces grated cheddar cheese
1 cup green onions, finely chopped
2 ounces crawfish fat
1/2 teaspoon Tabasco
1-cup water
3 cups cooked rice
Salt to taste

Melt butter and sauté green onions and celery for 15 minutes. Add fat and cook 5 minutes. Add soup, black, red and white pepper and Tabasco. Cook 5 minutes. Add crawfish tails, rice and water. Stir, making sure mixture is not too dry or runny. Add a little water if too dry. It must be thick enough to stand as a slice of pie. Add salt to taste. Stir in cheese and put in pie shell. Bake at 350 degrees for 15 minutes.

Serves 4 to 6.

(Miss Celeste tells me you can use shrimp if you like)

Carencro Meat Pie

2 tablespoons cooking oil
1 large onion, thinly sliced
1 bell pepper, chopped fine
1 pound lean ground meat
1 pound ground pork OR 1 pound meat dressing mix
1 cup potatoes, mashed
Cajun seasoning salt to taste
Pastry for double-crust pie
1 egg, beaten, for glaze on top crust

Preheat oven to 375 degrees. In skillet heat oil over medium burner. Sauté' onion and bell pepper until tender. Remove and set aside. Brown beef and pork together. Drain. Combine onion, bell pepper, meat, potatoes and seasoning.

Line pie plate with pastry. Fill with meat mixture. Top with crust. Seal and flute edges. Make slits in top of crust. Brush with beaten egg, if desired. Bake at 375°F for 30-35 minutes or until golden brown.

Serves 8-10

Carencro is a town near Lafayette and the folks there can sure cook!

St. Martinville Stuffed Onions

8 med. onions, peeled and parboiled
1 cup cooked, drained mixed vegetables
1 cup grated Comté cheese
1 cup med. white sauce
Salt, pepper, melted butter
White Sauce:
2 tablespoons butter
1 1/2 to 2 tablespoons flour
1 cup milk or light stock and cream

Parboil the onions and remove the center leaving the root end intact. Dice the center and add it to the mixed vegetables. Prepare the white sauce by melting the butter, then stirring in the flour over low heat for 3 to 4 minutes until well blended and there is no raw flour taste. Slowly stir in the milk. Simmer and stir the sauce with a wire whisk until it has thickened and is smooth and hot.

Add the cup of grated Comté cheese to cooked, drained mixed vegetables. Fill the onions and place them in a buttered baking dish. Sprinkle some Comté cheese on the top of each onion. Bake at 350°F until tender and browned.

St. Martinville is home to the legendary "Evangeline Oak;" made famous by the epic poem : "Evangeline", by American Poet, Henry Wadsworth Longfellow.

St. Gabriel Crawfish Stuffing

1/4 cup butter or margarine
1 tablespoon flour
1/2 cup onion, minced
1 tablespoon garlic, minced
1/2 cup parsley, chopped
1/2 teaspoon Salt
1/2 teaspoon black pepper
1/2 teaspoon cayenne pepper
1 egg, beaten
4 cups white bread, chopped
4 cups breadcrumbs
2 pounds crawfish tails, chopped

Melt butter in large saucepan; add flour and stir over heat until light brown. Add onion and garlic; sauté, and remove from heat; add parsley, seasonings, egg, chopped bread and crawfish tails and stir until mixed.

And we're all done.

Pasta St. Pierre
(An Elegant Cajun Original)

4 cups cooked angel hair pasta
2 cups cooked crawfish tails
2 slices of Canadian bacon
2 cups uncooked spinach
1 tablespoon fresh basil
1 ounce (Blush) wine
1 tablespoon fresh lime juice
1 tablespoon fresh lemon juice
1 cup Half and Half
1 cup sliced mushrooms
1/4 cup chopped fresh chives
1 tablespoon minced garlic
1/2 cup diced tomatoes
1/4 cup diced yellow bell pepper
2 tablespoon chopped fresh parsley
2 tablespoons pine nuts
1 teaspoon mint
1/2 teaspoon lemon pepper
All that Jazz Cajun & Creole Blast, to taste

Cook the Canadian bacon, remove bacon and cook the mushrooms, chives, garlic and tomato in grease. Sauté for 4-6 minutes. Add crawfish tails, yellow bell pepper, basil and return the Canadian bacon. Add wine, lemon and lime juice. Keep cooking on medium heat until liquids are reduced to half the original amount.

Add Half and Half, stir continually as you reduce the mixture over medium heat until it is a sauce. Now remove the saucepan from the heat. Add spinach, mint, lemon pepper, pine nuts and parsley. (Mix well)

Pour onto Angel Hair Pasta and add All That Jazz Cajun Blast to taste and garnish with 3 fresh slices of lime & 3 fresh slices of lemon.

I think you guys out there should make this dish for that special little lady in your life, just to show her how much you appreciate all that she does for you! (While you're at it throw in some candlelight and a good bottle of wine!)

Sauce Piquant and Alligator Stew

What's for breakfast I'm asking you?
Andouille with eggs and Boudin too!

What's for lunch? Oh tell me true.
Fish Courtbouillon and some Gasper Goo!

What's for supper? I wish I knew.
Sauce Piquant and Alligator Stew!

What's for dessert when we get through?
A nice Bread pudding and Pain Perdu!

Andouille (on-dooie)

LeBlanc's Alligator Sauce Piquant

4 pounds cubed alligator meat
1/2 cup chopped celery
1-cup flour
1/2 cup chopped bell pepper
1-cup oil
8 ounce can chopped mushrooms
4 tablespoons butter
1-cup water
2 medium chopped onions
1-jar salad olives
1/2 teaspoons sugar
1/4 cup chopped parsley
1 can tomato paste
1/4 cup chopped scallions
To taste salt & cayenne pepper

Soak meat with Tabasco and lemon juice for 30 minutes prior to cooking. Rinse before cooking. Make roux with 1-cup oil and 1-cup flour and cook until golden. Sauté onions in roux until brown. Add tomato paste and sugar and cook about 5 minutes. Add bell pepper, celery, garlic, and mushrooms; stir well. Add water and cook 1 hour over low heat.

Add scallions, parsley, alligator (cut in small pieces, and preferably meat other than from the tail) salt, pepper and cayenne to taste. Cover pot and cook slowly for 30 minutes or until meat is tender.

Add olives, which have been soaked in water and cook a few minutes longer. Serve over cooked rice.

Serves 8.

Don't say "GROSS" until you at least try it...This one is REALLY good!

Frog Legs Sauce Piquante

8 frog legs, cleaned
1/2-cup flour, well seasoned
3/4 cup vegetable shortening
2 garlic cloves, minced
1 onion, medium, thinly sliced
1 can tomatoes (16ounces)
Water
Salt
Cayenne pepper
1-cup parsley chopped
Green onion tops (chopped)

Dredge frog legs in seasoned flour; tap off excess flour and reserve.
Heat shortening in large skillet; sauté frog legs until well done. With
slotted spoon, remove legs; add reserved flour to skillet and cook,
stirring, until golden.

Add garlic and onion; cook, stirring, until vegetables are soft. Add
tomatoes and stir until oil floats on top. Add water to desired
consistency and season lightly. Add frog legs to sauce; simmer 10
minutes. Add parsley and onion tops just before serving.

(As a child I recall crying for the poor froggies… "Mama they
might need their legs!"
I also remember how the legs would jump in the pan while
cooking; reflex I suppose.)

Duplantier Crawfish Etouffee
(Pronounced A 2 Fay)

2 pounds crawfish tails
1/4 cup Oil
1 cup chopped onions
2 tablespoons crawfish fat (or more)
2 teaspoons cornstarch
1/4 cup parsley, chopped
1/4 pound margarine
1/2 cup chopped celery
4 cloves garlic, chopped fine
2 cups cold water
1/4 cup chopped green onion tops
Salt, red & black pepper

Season crawfish and set aside. Melt margarine, add seasoning, stirring constantly. Add crawfish and 1-1/2 cups water. Bring to boil, lower heat and cook slowly 30 minutes, stirring occasionally. Dissolve cornstarch in remaining 1/2 cup. water. Add to mixture.

Add onion tops and parsley. Cook for an additional 10 minutes.

Serves 4.

(This is also one of the all time favorite South Louisiana Dishes!)

Churchpoint Chicken Etouffee

3/4-cup onion, half fine cut half rough cut.
3/4-cup bell pepper, fine cut.
3/4-cup celery, fine cut.
3 little green onions, fine chop.
1 large clove garlic, fine chop.
2 teaspoon Cajun chicken spice mixture.
3 pats butter.
3 tablespoon dry roux.
3 cups chicken broth.
2 chicken breasts.

Pre cook the chicken breasts in microwave for about 10 minutes on high. Set aside to cool. When cool, pull into strips about the size of a small finger. (You could use an equal amount of leftover roast chicken.)

Singe the rough-cut onions in cast iron skillet over medium high heat. When lightly browned (3-5 minutes). Add the rest of the vegetables, the garlic and the spices. Add butter and sizzle over medium heat until the vegetables are limp, about 5 minutes. Stir in the dry roux. Then stir in the chicken broth and simmer uncovered over low heat for 15 minutes. Add the chicken and continue to simmer for another 10-15 minutes. The sauce should be about as thick as a thin gravy.

Serve over rice.

Makes 2 generous servings.

SHRIMP ETOUFFEE Follow same recipe except: use one small package shrimp (5-6ounces) decrease vegetable amounts to 1/2 cup each. Decrease spice amount to 1 teaspoon Cajun chicken mix. Decrease roux to 2 tablespoon decrease butter to 2 pats decrease broth to 1 cup do not pre-cook shrimp.

At the end, add uncooked shrimp and simmer for only 2-3 minutes.

(Highly recommended by Mrs. Boudreaux, pronounced "Boo-Drow")

Marksville Dirty Rice

1/2 Pound ground beef
5 chicken livers, 5 chicken gizzards-chopped.
Salt and pepper to taste
Cayenne pepper to taste
1-tablespoon butter
1 cup parsley—chopped
1 1/2 cups green onions —chopped
2 cups regular rice —uncooked
4 1/2 cups chicken broth

Season beef, livers and gizzards with salt and cayenne pepper. Cook in butter, stirring to crumble, until browned. Add parsley and green onion. Cook until vegetables are softened. Stir in rice and add broth. Bring to a boil, reduce heat and simmer for 1 hour. Sprinkle surface of rice with black pepper before serving. For variety, use 1-cup wild rice with 1-cup regular rice.

Serves 8

The humorous name of this dish came about because of the appearance of the white rice, liver and gizzards, when combined. God it is good!

Cajun Yaya
(Yaya is the African word for rice)

½ cup vegetable oil
½ cup flour
1 pound ground beef
1 pound ground pork
½ pound ground pork liver
1 red bell pepper, chopped
3 yellow onions, chopped
3 stalks celery, chopped
1-1/2 cups water
1 jalapeno pepper, chopped
6-8 green onion tops, chopped
½ cup minced fresh parsley
1 teaspoon celery seed
1 teaspoon All That Jazz Cajun & Creole Blast
3 cups cooked rice

Make a light brown roux with oil and flour. Sauté beef, pork, and liver in separate pot until brown; add red bell pepper, yellow onions, and celery, and keep cooking until onions are transparent. Add roux and water to meat mixture and simmer for 40 minutes. Add All That Jazz Cajun & Creole Blast, cayenne pepper, green onion tops, and fresh parsley, and mix well. Add cooked rice once you are ready to serve, and stir it up well.

New Iberia, Louisiana is home to America's oldest rice mill... "Konriko!"

Mambo Oyster Dressing

4 tablespoons corn oil
2 tablespoons flour
1 large onion, chopped
1/2 bell pepper, chopped
2 cloves garlic, minced
1 cup chopped celery
1 quart raw oysters, drained
4 cups cooked white rice
1/4 cup minced parsley
1/2 cup minced green onion tops
Salt and black pepper to taste

Heat corn oil in heavy skillet. Gradually add flour, stirring constantly for 6 minutes. Add onions, bell pepper, garlic, and celery; stir and cook until tender Add oysters. Cook until oysters curl.

Remove skillet from heat. Add rice, parsley, green onion tops, and seasonings. Mix well. Serve hot as a side dish or use to stuff chickens, turkeys or ducks.

Serves 8.

This was one of Jazz Great, Louie "Satchmo" Armstrong's Favorites!

T-Coon

T-Coon, T-Coon, Married last June,
His wife wore white but he wore maroon.
T-Coon, T-Coon, was back so soon,
Saw him dancing with a big baboon.

T-Coon did you hear what I just said?
He laughs at chickens running with no head!
T-Coon did you hear what I just told?
He thinks ice is hot and fire is cold!

T-Coon he is one crazy old man;
Likes frog-legs jumping in the frying pan!
T-Coon he is a really strange guy;
Says Merry Christmas on the fourth of July!

T-Coon, T-Coon, that silly loon,
Hear him howling at the Cajun moon!
T-Coon, T-Coon, quarter passed noon,
Eating catfish with a gumbo spoon…

T-Coon's Shrimp Creole

2 pounds fresh shrimp — (Peeled and deveined)
1/2 cup vegetable oil
2 large bell peppers — chopped
10 large tomatoes — peeled & seeded
1 teaspoon ground red pepper
1/2 teaspoon ground white pepper
1-tablespoon fresh basil dried
5 bay leaves
1 cup parsley — chopped
3 med. yellow onions — chopped
5 celery ribs — chopped fine
2 teaspoons salt
1/2 teaspoon ground black pepper
1-tablespoon fresh thyme dried
1 1/2 teaspoons   sugar
1 cup green onions — chopped

Peel and devein the shrimp. Place heads (if you have them), and peels in a small saucepan and add the water. Bring to a slow boil over medium-high heat and let boil slowly for 15-20 minutes. Strain and discard the heads and peels.

Place the oil in a Dutch oven or other large, heavy pot and place over medium-high heat. Add the onions, peppers, and celery and sauté stirring often, until the vegetables are very soft, about 45 minutes. Stir in the tomatoes, salt, peppers, herbs, sugar, and shrimp stock and return to simmer. Reduce heat to medium and let simmer for 2 hours, stirring occasionally.

This is your Creole sauce; it can be prepared 1 or 2 days in advance and stored in the refrigerator (I find the sauce is even better after sitting a couple of days in the refrigerator). When you are ready to serve, return the sauce to a simmer and add the shrimp. Cook until they turn pink, 5-7 minutes. Stir in the green onions and parsley and let cook for 1 minute more. Serve on flat plates over beds of rice.

Serves 6-8

To date, this is the BEST Shrimp Creole I have ever tasted!

Cousin Camille's Shrimp Creole Salad

1 pound shrimp (peeled and deveined)
1 large garlic clove
4 celery tops
2 ribs celery, finely chopped
1 hard-boiled egg finely chopped
1 small sweet pickle finely chop
1 teaspoon chopped hot peppers
2 tablespoons mayonnaise
Salt to taste
Cayenne pepper (to taste)
Lettuce leaves
Avocado halves
Whole tomatoes

Drop shrimp, garlic and celery tops into boiling water; boil for about 15 minutes. Cut each piece of shrimp into 2 or 3 pieces. Combine chopped celery, egg, pickle, hot peppers, mayonnaise and shrimp; mix thoroughly, adding salt and cayenne to taste.

Serve on lettuce leaves or use to fill avocado halves or hollowed tomatoes.

Serves 6

Avocado is not a traditional item found in Cajun Cooking, but Cousin Camille insisted I include it!

Mi Mi's Red Snapper

Stuffed And Baked
1 large onion, chopped
2 cloves garlic, minced
1/2 cup diced celery
5 tablespoons butter
1 tablespoon minced parsley
1/2 cup chopped mushrooms
1/2 cup chopped fresh tomatoes
1/2 cup chopped cooked oysters
1/2 cup crabmeat, flaked
1 cup boiled shrimp, chopped
1/2-teaspoon salt
1 teaspoon Tabasco
Dried breadcrumbs
1 large egg, beaten
1 5-pound red snapper, dressed

Stir and cook onion, garlic, and celery in butter until wilted. Mix together remaining ingredients, except for egg. Use breadcrumbs to make a slightly dry mixture. Add egg; mix well. Stuff snapper lightly; securing with skewers. Place snapper into greased baking dish. Season outside with salt and Tabasco. Baste often with butter. Bake in a 350-degree oven for 40 minutes. Serve with rice.

Serves 6.

Mi Mi passed away in 1999 at the age of 97, but she lives on through the wonderful recipes she handed down for generations!

Jazzy Crawfish Bisque

1-1/2 cup crawfish tails
1/4 cup cooking oil
1/4 cup all-purpose flour
1 small onion, chopped
1 stick celery, chopped
1 clove garlic, mashed
1 bay leaf
3/4 cup tomatoes, chopped
1-1/2 pint cold water
1 pint cold water mixed with 1/2 cup crawfish fat
1 teaspoon salt
1/4 teaspoon sugar
1/4 teaspoon red pepper
1/2 teaspoon Tabasco
1 tablespoon green onion
1 tablespoon chopped parsley

In a heavy bottomed pot, make roux by adding flour to heated oil, over low heat, stir constantly until a deep golden brown; take pot away from heat; add onion, garlic and celery. Cook for 5 minutes; stir and return to heat.

Add 1 pint of water, tomatoes, sugar, salt and pepper; cook over high heat, stirring until sauce simmers; then reduce heat again. As sauce simmers, combine remaining water with crawfish fat in saucepan, cook over high heat, stirring constantly until it comes to a boil.

Add sauce to fat and water, let simmer for 1 hour. Season with salt and pepper and Tabasco. Add crawfish tails, green onion and parsley. Serve in soup bowl over a scoop of rice.

Serves 4.

A tried and true method!

Coonass Cornbread
Easy 1-2-3 Method

2 eggs + 3 egg whites
4 cups yellow corn meal
6 teaspoons baking powder
1 teaspoon All That Jazz Cajun Seasoning
1 cup cream style corn
2 cups 1% milk
2 tablespoons melted butter or margarine
4 teaspoons sugar
4 ounces extra sharp cheddar cheese, shredded
2 cups crawfish tails

1) Combine all ingredients and mix

2) Bake at 375 degrees for exactly 1 hour

3) Serve plain or topped with crawfish etouffee

Also goes well with grilled mahi-mahi.

Note: According to the dictionary Coonass is…"n. Offensive Slang
Used as a disparaging term for a Cajun."
It was obviously a non-Cajun that wrote that definition. Being
that we often call each other Coonasses, in fact I'd go so far as to
say it has become a term of endearment! But that doesn't mean it's
OK to call me that if I don't know you and your intention is to
disrespect my Acadian heritage!

Creole Cabbage Rolls

12 cabbage leaves,
Cut large ones in half along ridge
3 tablespoons bacon grease or sausage drippings
1 clove garlic, finely minced
1/2 pound ground beef
1/2 of a well beaten egg
1/2 teaspoon red pepper
1 small onion, chopped
3/4 cup cooked rice
1 teaspoon salt

Cook onion and garlic in bacon grease until tender. In large bowl, mix meat, rice, egg, salt, pepper and cooked onion. Place 1 tablespoon of the mixture into the soft end of the cabbage, ending with the large end of the leaf. Continue until all are rolled.

In saucepan that has a tight fitting lid, place a pan rack, crumbled foil, or pieces of cabbage on bottom and add water. Place rolls hard end down.

Sauce:

1 cup canned whole tomatoes and juice
1/2 teaspoon red pepper
1/2 lemon (for juice)
1 teaspoon salt
1 teaspoon sugar
1 cup water

Combine tomatoes, salt, sugar and pepper. Pour over cabbage. Squeeze lemon over all. Cover with a tight fitting lid. Cook 15 minutes, then reduce heat to low. Cook 50 minutes more.

Serves 2.

I make these at least twice a month for friends and family!

My Pirogue

My little pirogue may be slow,
But, there's no need to worry.
It gets me where I need to go,
Besides I'm in no hurry.

It could be newer or faster,
This raggedy boat of mine
Sure knows this Atchafalaya,
Yet, no longer does it shine.

My little pirogue may be slow,
Still, it suits me to a tee.
It gets me where I need to go,
Hey, that's good enough for me!

Pirogue: A canoe made from a hallowed tree-trunk.
Atchafalaya: A river of south-central Louisiana.

Real Red Beans and Rice

2 pounds Dried red kidney beans
2 cups Chopped yellow onions
1 bunch of scallions, chopped
3 or 4 finely sliced cloves-of garlic
1 bunch Parsley (chopped)
3 pounds smoked sausage
Salt and pepper to taste
3 quarts of cold water
1 ham bone

Soak beans overnight if possible. Drain water and add beans to a large 8 or 10-quart pot. Then add enough of the cold water to cover the beans. Add chopped yellow onions and garlic and bring to a boil. Cook for one hour and add all the other things and more water if necessary.

Simmer for 2 more hours or until the beans are soft. Then remove 2 cups of cooked beans without juice and mash good. Then return the mashed up beans to the pot and stir into the mixture. This makes a creamy, thicker gravy. Served over rice.

Serves 8.

(I like a good bit of Tabasco drizzled on top of mine.)

White Bean Creole Soup
(The Easy Way Out)

1/2 cup minced onion
1/2 cup minced celery
1/4 cup chopped bell pepper
2 tablespoons butter or margarine
1 1/2 pounds ham, 1" cubes
1 pound smoked sausage, 1/2" slices
1 can tomato sauce (8 ounces)
2 cans navy beans w/bacon (16 ounces)
4 cups water
Salt
Black pepper

In large saucepan, cook onion, celery and bell pepper in butter until soft. Add ham and tomato sauce; simmer 15 to 20 minutes. In separate saucepan, bring navy beans with bacon to boil. Puree beans and their liquid in a food processor or blender; add to ham mixture. Add the water; season to taste and simmer for 1 hour. Serve piping hot.

Serves 6

(Good February food, since it doesn't get cold too much in South Louisiana)

Bertrand's Boudin

3 cups water
1/2 pound boneless pork, cubed
1/8 pound pork liver
1/2 cup onion, chopped
1/4 cup green onion, chopped
1 teaspoon parsley-flakes
1 teaspoon celery-flakes
3/4 teaspoon salt
1/2 teaspoon black pepper
3/4 teaspoon red pepper
3/4 cup cooked rice
Sausage casing

Place water, boneless pork, and pork liver in a 2-quart saucepan. Bring mixture to a boil over high heat. Reduce to a medium heat setting and simmer until pork is tender.

Remove pork and liver from stock. Grind pork and liver (use food processor, if desired). Add onion, green onion and other seasonings to stock. Cook until onions are tender. Add ground meat to vegetable-stock mixture. Cook until most of the water has evaporated. Stir in cooked rice. Adjust seasonings, if desired.

Stuff rice-meat mixture into sausage casings. Prick casings 3-4 times each to prevent bursting during cooking. Cook boudin in simmering water for 12 minutes. Remove from water and serve.

(Yields 18 inches of this Cajun Favorite)

Catfish Courtbouillon

2 large catfish fillets (or any firm fish)
1 cup onions, chopped fine
1/2 cup celery, chopped fine
2 garlic cloves, minced
1/3-cup butter
1/3-cup flour
1 teaspoon salt
1/2-teaspoon black pepper
1/4-teaspoon cayenne pepper (or more, -for real Cajun flavor)
3 large tomatoes, peeled and quartered (or use about a 1 pound can of tomatoes)
3 cups water
2 cups rice (cooked) hot

In a deep skillet or Dutch oven mix the butter and flour together over low heat to form a roux (a thick, smooth, bubbly mixture). Add the onions, celery and garlic and sauté until tender. Add the tomatoes, salt, pepper, cayenne and water. Simmer covered for 20-30 minutes.

Add fillets and cook until tender and flaky, 15-20 minutes. Serve on a bed of rice.

The amount of cayenne here is set for a mildly hot taste. It can be increased up to a full teaspoon for the real version!

Catfish Courtbouillon; (pronounced coo-be-yon) a popular Cajun meal!

Belle Rose Stuffed Mirlitons

4 medium mirlitons
1-1/2 cups bread crumbs
5 tablespoons butter
2 cloves garlic, minced
1 large Vidalia onion, finely chopped
1 pound shrimp, coarsely chopped
1 teaspoon salt
1 teaspoon Tabasco
1 egg well beaten
3 teaspoons chopped, fresh parsley
1/2 teaspoon ground thyme
3/4 cup Italian breadcrumbs

Let mirlitons simmer in salt water until tender and then let them cool. Cut each in half and remove seeds. Scoop out pulp. Coarsely chop the pulp. Drain excess water and add breadcrumbs. Melt butter in large skillet, sauté garlic and onion over medium heat for 5 minutes.

Add the chopped shrimp, cook ten minutes. Add mirliton pulp mixture, salt and Tabasco sauce. Taste and correct seasoning if necessary. Cook for 5 more minutes, stirring constantly. Allow mixture to cool; then add beaten egg, parsley and thyme.

Mix until all ingredients are thoroughly blended. Fill the mirliton skins with mixture. Sprinkle top of each with Italian breadcrumbs. Brush tops generously with butter. Bake in 375-degree oven for 30 minutes.

Serves 6 to 8.

In California & Florida Mirliton is called Chayote (shy-otie),
in the Caribbean, it is known as Chouchou. It is also
known as vegetable pear, mango squash and Aztec squash.
Eggplants may be substituted for mirliton.

Houseboat
(Through the Eyes of a Child)

Oh if I lived on a houseboat,
I could fish from my own front door.
I'd have to watch out for gators,
And snakes on my living room floor.

Oh if I lived on a houseboat,
I'm sure I would like it, I think.
I'd have etouffee everyday.
A turtle would live in my sink.

Oh if I lived on a houseboat,
My friends could all visit each night.
For now, it's just wishful thinking.
But when I get older... I MIGHT!

Terrebonne Wild Baked Ducks

2 wild ducks, dressed
Salt, red and black pepper
1 large onion, halved
1 large onion, chopped
2 stalks of celery, halved
1/2 cup cooking oil
1-1/2 cups chicken stock
1 cup sherry wine
1 tablespoon flour
1/2 cup water
4 teaspoons chopped parsley

Season the ducks inside and out with salt and pepper. Put onion and celery into the cavity of each duck. (If they would have brushed, they wouldn't have cavities).

Heat oil in heavy Dutch oven; brown ducks. Add chopped onion; stir and cook until wilted. Add 1-cup water and sherry wine. Cover and cook at 350 degrees for 2-1/2 hours. Baste frequently. Add additional water as needed.

Once they are cooked remove ducks to a platter. Mix flour with a little water, stir into drippings to make a thin gravy. Stir in the parsley. Serve with wild rice.

Serves 8.

Daffy & Donald would have had very short lives around here!

Crawfish Fettuccine: From a Lady in Gretna

1-1/2 cups butter
3 medium onions, chopped
3 ribs celery, chopped
2 bell peppers, chopped
1/4-cup flour
1/3-cup parsley flakes
2 pounds of peeled crawfish tails
1-pint half-and-half
1/2 cup white wine
1 pound Velveeta cheese, in 1/2-inch cubes
2 tablespoons chopped jalapeno peppers
3 cloves of garlic, crushed
Creole Seasoning
1 pound fettuccine noodles
1 tablespoon olive oil
1/2 cup Parmesan cheese

Melt butter in heavy skillet. Add onions, celery and bell peppers. Cook 12 minutes. Add flour and blend well. Cover and cook 15 minutes over low heat. Stirring occasionally. Add parsley and crawfish tails. Cover and cook 20 minutes, stirring often. Add half-and-half, wine, cheese, jalapenos and garlic. Mix well. Add Creole seasoning to taste. Cook noodles until done. Drain and add one tablespoon of olive oil and Parmesan cheese. Combine both mixtures and pour into a 3-quart buttered casserole. Bake at 350 for 10 minutes.

Serves 12-16

There are many recipes for this dish, but this one reigns supreme!

Cordon Bleu With Pecan Crust

6 boneless chicken breasts
6 to 8 ounces of thinly sliced beef
8 ounces of shredded swiss cheese
4 tablespoons butter
1/2-cup buttermilk
1 large egg
1 cup all-purpose flour
1 cup pecans (ground)
1/4-cup sesame seeds
1 tablespoon paprika
2 teaspoons salt
1/4 teaspoon pepper

Pound chicken breasts thin. Top with ham and Swiss cheese; roll and secure with a toothpick. Preheat oven to 375. Place butter in a large pan. Melt butter in hot oven.
Mix buttermilk with egg in a small mixing bowl. In a large plastic bag, combine the remaining ingredients, mixing thoroughly. Dip chicken in buttermilk mixture. Place into plastic bag and shake. Place chicken in pan with melted butter, turning to coat. Bake for one hour.

Serves 6 or 3 if they want seconds; and they will!

Mr. Robichaux's Cajun Blossom
(Pronounced: Row-ba-show)

1 large Vidalia onion
2 Tablespoons all-purpose flour
1 large egg, lightly beaten
1 cup saltine cracker crumbs
vegetable oil
1/2 Tablespoon salt
Tabasco
Dark honey mustard or ranch dressing

Peel onion, leaving root end intact. Cut into fourths, cutting to within 1/2 inch of the root end. Cut fourths into thirds. Place onion in boiling water for 1 minute; remove and place in ice water for 5 minutes. Loosen petals if necessary. Drain onion, cut side down. Place flour in a Ziploc bag; add onion, shaking to coat.

Dip onion in egg. Place cracker crumbs into Ziploc and add onion, tossing to coat. Chill for 1 hour. Pour oil to a depth of 3 inches into electric fryer or heavy saucepan and heat to 375.

Fry onion for 5 to 7 minutes or until golden brown; drain on paper towels. Sprinkle with salt and drizzle with Tabasco. Serve appetizer with dressing.

Too yummy to serve more than 2.

Zydeco Chicken

6 chicken breasts, boned and skinned
1/2 cup flour, seasoned with salt and pepper
1/2 cup butter
1/2 cup oil
8 ounces mushrooms, sliced
1-1/2 cups chopped green onions
3 tomatoes, peeled and diced
4 cloves garlic, minced
1 pinch tarragon
8 ounces white wine
1 cup chicken stock
1 teaspoon cornstarch dissolved in 1-tablespoon water
Parsley for garnish

Coat chicken with flour mixture. Put chicken into hot skillet with oil and butter and lightly brown both sides. Remove chicken.

Lower heat and cook sliced mushrooms for five minutes, stirring often. Add green onions and cook for 5 minutes, stirring often. Add tomatoes, garlic, and tarragon and cook 15 minutes, stirring occasionally. Add white wine and chicken stock. Cook for five more minutes. Add cornstarch dissolved in water to the sauce. Stir well.

Return chicken to pan and cook in sauce for 20 minutes. Add parsley and serve.

Serves 6.

(Zah-dee-ko) is the most contemporary expression of Black Creole music. It is said to have originated from many sources, but the influence of the blues and soul music is significant in its development. Zydeco is translated to mean "Snap Bean" and can be played on accordions, metal washboards, thimbles, spoons and bottle openers.

INVITATION

Come on down to da Bayou Bridge you,
When you come to da bluff take a right.
It's the third house passed Pecan Ridge you,
Oh, we're boiling dim blue crab tonight.

You can bring Boo and Mister Pecou.
Bring your Grandson who still keeps in touch.
But don't you bring that Lou Lanoux,
Cuz I find dat she eats way too much!

The skies are clear and summer is here.
The mosquitoes are starting to bite.
Come on down to da Bayou Bridge you,
Oh, were boiling dim blue crab tonight.

Some words in the above poem are deliberately misspelled
for phonetic/humorous effect.

Bertile's Crab Meat AU Gratin

1 medium onion, minced
1/2 cup minced celery
2 tablespoons butter
1/2-cup flour
5-ounces evaporated milk
2 egg yolks, beaten
Salt and Tabasco to taste
1 pound lump crabmeat
1/2-pound cheddar cheese, grated

Stir and cook onion and celery in butter until tender. Stir in flour, blending well. Stir in milk. Stir in egg yolks. Add salt, Tabasco and crab meat. Blend well. Put mixture into a greased oblong glass casserole dish. Top with cheese. Bake in a 375-degree oven for 15 minutes.

Serves 4.

(Fake crabmeat is NOT recommended!)

Lake Charles Stuffed Crabs

1 cup chopped onions
1/2 cup bell peppers
1/2 cup chopped celery
8 tablespoons butter
1 pound fresh crabmeat
6 slices bread, toasted
1 cup evaporated milk
1/2 teaspoon Worcestershire
3 eggs beaten
Salt and Tabasco to taste
1 tablespoon minced parsley
1/2 cup minced green onion tops
Dry breadcrumbs

Stir and cook onion, bell pepper, and celery in butter until tender. Add crabmeat; cook 5 minutes. Soak toasted bread in milk; squeeze milk out; add bread and remaining milk to crab mixture. Add balance of ingredients, except dry breadcrumbs; mix well. Put into 12 clean crab shells. Top with dry breadcrumbs. Dot with additional butter. Bake in 375-degree oven for 15 minutes, or until piping hot.

Serves 6.

(Some friends over near the Texas border taught me this one. Thanks René & T-Joe!)

Cheramie's Marinated Crabs

2 dozen fresh crabs, boiled and cleaned
2 cups Italian dressing
1/2 cup olive oil
1/2 cup wine vinegar
1/2 cup finely chopped celery
1 cup green onions, chopped finely
6 cloves, garlic, chopped finely
1/2 cup chopped dill pickles
1/2 cup fresh shrimp, cooked and cleaned
1-1/2 teaspoon Tabasco sauce
Salt to taste

Cut crabs in half; remove claws. Combine all ingredients except crab and shrimp, mixing marinade well. Place crabs, claws and shrimp in large bowl. Pour marinade over all.
Refrigerate for at least 12 hours.

Serves 6

(This one came from a restaurant in Grand Isle)

Cajun Crab Dip

3 tablespoons butter
4 tablespoons minced onion
1 cup fresh mushrooms, sliced, cooked, drained
1/4 cup all-purpose flour
1-1/4 cups milk
Couple dashes of Tabasco
1/2 teaspoon salt
Black pepper to taste
1/2 teaspoon prepared mustard
1 cup cheddar cheese, grated
1 pound fresh crabmeat

Heat butter in saucepan. Add onions; stir and cook until wilted.
Add mushrooms; stir and cook 2 minutes. Add flour; blend well.
Stir in milk, Tabasco, salt, pepper, and mustard.
Add cheese; blend until melted. Add crabmeat; simmer until
cooked.

Serves 10.

Great Pig-out Party Food!

Zulu Crab & Corn Bisque

4 ounces real butter
2 med. onions, chopped
2 cup flour
1 pound white crab meat
1 can whole kernel corn
1 can cream style corn
2 cups milk
2 cup water
1 qt. cream
1 1/2 tablespoons chicken base
1/2 tablespoon white pepper
All That Jazz Cajun & Creole Blast
cornstarch roux (2 tablespoons cornstarch and 3/4 cup water)
1/8 cup parsley flakes
1/8 cup green onions, chopped

Sauté onions in butter, add flour and mix well, letting simmer for 5 minutes. Add corn, crabmeat, milk, cream, chicken base, white pepper and All That Jazz Cajun & Creole Blast. Let cook for 15 minutes.

Add cornstarch roux and simmer for 10 minutes. Add parsley flakes, onion tops and 2 cups water. Cook an additional 5 minutes and serve.

A Crescent City Classic!

Simple Truth

Come pass yourself a good time,
Come sail the Pontchartrain.
Old Man River can still deliver
Magic that's sweet like sugarcane.

There's charm and style in a Cajun smile,
Simple, the truth that remains...
I'm a believer in Cajun fever,
There's Café au Lait in my veins!

Pontchartrain: A lake of Southeast Louisiana, north of New
Orleans.

Everyday CAFÉ AU LAIT

3 tablespoons sugar
3 cups light cream or milk
2 cups hot fresh coffee

Heat sugar in heavy saucepan until caramelized. Remove from heat and place in a bowl.
Heat cream or milk over low heat; beat with an eggbeater until it foams. Pour into a serving pot. Put sugar in serving cups; Pour equal amounts of hot coffee and hot cream or milk over sugar.

Serves 4

French Market Doughnuts
(AKA Beignets)

1 cup milk
2 tablespoons margarine
4 tablespoons sugar
1/2-teaspoon salt
1 egg, beaten
3 cups all-purpose flour
1 packet yeast

Heat milk over low heat. Add margarine, sugar, and salt; Stir well; cool to lukewarm. Stir in egg. In large bowl combine 1-1/2 cups flour and yeast. Add milk mixture; beat 5 minutes. Gradually add remaining flour. Form dough into a ball; place in greased bowl; turn to coat. Cover; chill in refrigerator for 4 hours. Pat out dough on floured pastry cloth.
Cover and let stand for 15 minutes. Roll out to form triangles-3x2-inch size is best. Cover and let stand 25 minutes. Deep-fry beignets in corn oil, just a few at a time, until golden. Drain on paper towels. Sprinkle with powdered sugar.

Makes 3 dozen.

Serve with coffee that contains chicory or with Café Au Lait!

Once Upon A Mardi Gras
(A Childhood Remembrance)

Throw me something Mister,
Beads of purple, gold and green.
Throw six more for my sister
If you know just what I mean.

What if all these beads were REAL...
For ONE moment I pretended.
What if plastic could be jewels,
And Fat Tuesday never ended?

We stood and watched this world in awe,
My sister, me and Nanna.
Once upon a Mardi Gras
Right here in Louisiana.

Mardi Gras King Cake

Dough:
3-1/2 cups flour, sifted
1/4 cup sugar
1 package active dry yeast
1 teaspoon salt
1/2 cup water
1/2 cup milk
1/4 cup butter
1 egg

Filling:
1-1/4 cups brown sugar
2 teaspoons cinnamon
1/3-cup butter, softened

Icing:
1 cup confectioners sugar
1 teaspoon vanilla
2 tablespoons milk
1 teaspoon oil

In a large mixing bowl, mix 1-cup flour, sugar, yeast and salt. Place water, milk, and butter in saucepan over low heat until liquids are warm and butter is melted. Gradually add liquid to dry ingredients and beat with an electric mixer for 2 minutes at medium speed. Add egg and 1 cup of flour. Beat at high speed for 2 minutes. Add enough of the remaining flour to make a stiff dough.

Turn out onto a heavily floured board and knead 5 to 10 minutes until dough is smooth. Add flour to board as needed to prevent dough from sticking. Place ball of dough into greased bowl; turn once to bring greased side up. Cover with a damp cloth and let rise in a warm place until double in bulk (about 1-1/2 hours) Punch down, turn out onto a lightly floured board. Knead 6 times.

Divide dough in half. Roll half of the dough into a 25x15 inch oblong. Spread with 5 teaspoons softened butter. Sprinkle with half of the brown sugar and cinnamon mixture. Roll tightly, starting with wide side. Pinch the edges. Repeat procedure with the rest of the dough.

Twist the two rolls and attach ends. Place ring on greased baking sheet. Cover with greased waxed paper and towel. Let rise in warm place for 1-1/2 hours or until doubled. Place in a preheated 375 oven; bake for 30 minutes or until golden. After the King Cake cools, spread icing on top. Decorate with gold, purple and green sugars, Serves 12.

Icing: Combine sugar, vanilla, and milk. Beat for about 1 minute with electric mixer. Add oil and beat until creamy.

The King Cake is believed to have been brought to New Orleans, Louisiana, from France in the 1870s. A dried bean or pea was hidden inside the cake and the finder became king or queen for the day. Today a tiny doll or a single jellybean is hidden in the cake as the prize, and with it comes the obligation to host the next Mardi Gras party (or office treat) and provide the next King Cake.

Bring the Mardi Gras celebration to wherever you live! Bake a King Cake and start the tradition! This recipe may look long and complicated, but it really isn't, and you will have fun making it!

Did You Know.....

That the Royal Mardi Gras Colors were selected in 1872 for the
first Rex Parade in honor of the
Grand Duke Alexis' visit to New Orleans?
The PURPLE stands for JUSTICE,
The GREEN is for FAITH,
And the GOLD for POWER!

Small Town Mardi Gras

Big Mamou is calling you!
Bring your mother and brother- in -law.
Dozens of cousins going too,
Nothing like a small-town Mardi Gras.
If you want to know what Mardi Gras means;
You're not going to find it in New Orleans.
The real Fat Tuesday's our claim to fame,
Big city carnival's not the same.
Dozens of cousins going too,
Bring your Beau and bring your PawPaw.
Big Mamou is calling you!
Nothing like a small-town Mardi Gras.

Mamou: A town in South Louisiana famous for their "Small Town Mardi Gras." Well worth the trip!

Masked, costumed horsemen ride the Cajun countryside each Mardi Gras, stopping at rural farmhouses to ask in French for a chicken for the community gumbo.

Creole Wedding Rings

6 large Vidalia onions
1/4 cup butter
2 whole cloves
1/2 teaspoon garlic salt
1/4 teaspoon pepper
1 cup Burgundy wine

Cut onions into 1/4 inch slices and separate into rings. Melt butter in a large skillet, add the onions and cook, stirring until they are well coated. Add cloves, salt and pepper and sauté the onions until golden. Add the wine, cover and simmer for about 15 minutes. Discard the cloves. Remove the cover and cook onions until liquid is reduced almost to a glaze.

Serves 4.

Some married couples eat this dish on their anniversary to enhance passion and preserve fidelity.

Maque Choux

1/2 cup bacon drippings
35 ounces of canned corn (drained)
1 large onion, chopped
2 medium garlic cloves, minced
1 large green pepper, chopped
2 medium tomatoes, peeled/chopped
1 teaspoon salt
1/2 teaspoon black pepper
1 tablespoon sugar
1/2 teaspoon cayenne pepper
1 cup chicken broth, canned
1 cup milk
2 eggs

Heat bacon drippings in a heavy 12-inch skillet over medium heat. Add corn, onion, garlic, and bell pepper; cook until onion is thoroughly wilted and transparent, about 10 minutes. Stir often to prevent sticking. Add tomatoes, salt, black pepper, sugar and cayenne; stir until combined. Add broth. Reduce heat. Barely simmer, stirring often, until liquid has almost evaporated, about 30 minutes. The mixture will be thick and mushy.

Stir in milk; cook until reduced by 1/2. Increase heat slightly. In a small bowl, beat eggs until frothy; stirring constantly, add to pan in a slow steady stream. Cook just to thicken, 3 or 4 minutes. Serve hot.

Makes 4 to 6 servings.

(We'll save the health-nut stuff for another cookbook. This one is about flavor, my friend!)

St. Charles Stuffed Mushrooms

2 dozen large fresh mushrooms
4 tablespoons butter
2 cloves garlic, minced
3 tablespoons minced onion
1/2 pound cooked crabmeat
2 eggs, beaten
2 tablespoons mayonnaise
3 tablespoons seasoned minced green onion
1 teaspoon fresh lemon juice
Salt and pepper to taste
Parmesan cheese

Remove stems from mushrooms; chop stems and sauté in butter with garlic and onion. Brush mushrooms with melted butter. Mix together crabmeat, eggs, mayonnaise, breadcrumbs, green onion, lemon juice, salt and pepper, add to onion and garlic mixture and cook 6 minutes. Fill mushrooms with mixture. Sprinkle with cheese.

Bake in greased glass casserole dish for 15 minutes at 400-degrees.

Makes 2 dozen.

You wanna meet some nice folks? Go to St. Charles Parish!

General Lafayette Crawfish Puffs

12 frozen puff pastry shells
1-1/2 sticks butter
2 tablespoons crawfish fat, if desired
1 tablespoon tomato sauce
1/3 cup celery, chopped
1/4 cup bell pepper, chopped
2/3 cup onions, chopped
1 tablespoons. garlic, minced
1 pound crawfish tails, cleaned and deveined
1/4 tsp. coarsely ground black pepper
1/8 tsp. finely ground red pepper
1/2 tsp. salt
dash finely ground black pepper
1-1/2 heaping tsp. cornstarch
1-1/3 cup water
1/4 cup parsley, chopped
2 cup processed cheese, grated
1/4 cup sliced almonds, crushed
2 tablespoons parsley, chopped

Preheat oven to 350 degrees. Bake pastry shells according to package directions and set aside.

In deep heavy cooking pot, over medium-high heat, add butter and crawfish fat. Add tomato sauce, celery, bell peppers, onions and garlic, stirring frequently until tender. Add seasoning. Cook for 15 minutes.

In a separate bowl, add cornstarch and make a paste with a small amount of the water, gradually adding the remaining water. Add this water to the crawfish and continue cooking about five more minutes or until thickened. Add parsley, mix well, and then remove from stove.

Fill puffs equally with the crawfish filling. Top each puff with grated processed cheese. Top with crushed sliced almonds. Return filled puffs to oven and bake for a few more minutes to melt cheese. Remove from oven and sprinkle a small amount of the fresh parsley over each puff. Serve immediately.

Serves 6.

I first tasted this one at the Crawfish Festival in Breaux Bridge and I was hooked! (Breaux: Pronounced "Bro")

MudBug Salad

6 cups of Romaine lettuce, leaves separated and washed
Homemade Creole Honey Mustard Dressing (Instructions on next page)
2 cups of Crawfish tails
1 hard-boiled egg sliced
2 Tablespoons toasted sunflower seeds
1 small can sliced black olives
3-3/4 cup sliced mushrooms
1/3 cup green onions, sliced
1/4 cup roasted red belle peppers (in Jar)

Thinly slice 6 cups of Romaine lettuce leaves and put them into a large salad bowl.
Toss them with the Creole Honey Mustard Dressing (See Next Page) just enough to lightly coat.
Add remaining ingredients, including Crawfish meat,then add a little more dressing and toss.
Divide in equal portions in shallow individual bowls.

Creole Honey Mustard Dressing
(Simple & Sassy)

6 Tablespoons Creole Mustard (or brown mustard)
1-1/2 Tablespoon honey
1-1/2 Tablespoon freshly squeezed lemon juice
1/2 teaspoon olive oil
1/2 teaspoon All That Jazz Cajun Seasoning

Combine ingredients in a bowl and mix until completely blended!

Maybe I'm biased, but, I'm not alone when I tell you that Louisiana is high on the list when it comes to places that have the BEST cooking & eating on Earth!

But, don't take my word for it, just hop a flight to the Crescent City and decide for yourself!

And if you disagree after visiting the Big Easy I would only argue that you obviously didn't eat at the right places or that you should have let me cook for you and yours!

Fleur de Lis Chicken

1/2 pound crawfish
1/2 pound spinach
1/2 cup Ricotta cheese
1/2 tablespoon garlic, crushed
1/4 cup Parmesan cheese, grated
1 tablespoon oregano
Five 8 ounce deboned chicken breasts
1 cup heavy cream
1/2 cup chicken stock
1 teaspoon black pepper
1/4 cup green onions
1/2 cup entail, chopped and browned
1/2 cup mushrooms chopped

Preheat oven to 350 degrees. Place crawfish, chopped spinach, Ricotta cheese, garlic, parmesan cheese and oregano in bowl. Mix well.

Stuff chicken breasts and bake at 350°F for 35 minutes. Mix heavy cream, garlic, chicken stock pepper, and entail and mushrooms. Let simmer until sauce thickens, then add green onions. Pour into casserole dish over stuffed breasts and serve.

The Fais Dodo
(Pronounced: Fay Doe Doe)

Shake a leg Clairee,
Please dance with me,
As the Cajun fiddles play on.
To the Fais dodo,
Come on let's go,
We could dance till the night is gone.
I know that you're fond
Of Jolie Blonde.
Sweet Clairee may I have this dance?
The bands really good,
I wish you would
Give a poor Cajun a chance.
Hurry let's go
To the fais dodo.
Come join me! Well what do you say?
And if it's alright,
Tomorrow night;
Would you come to the Cochon De Lait?

Fais DoDo: A Cajun Dance Party.
Jolie Blonde: (Pretty Blonde) A song considered by many to be
"The Cajun National Anthem."
Cochon de Lait: A Party (Lasting at least 15 hours)
where a whole pig is roasted.

Cochon de Lait (Roasted Pig)
Yield - 100 -125 Buffet Servings

Ingredients
One 90 - 125 lbs head on pig (split lengthwise)
2 cups garlic toes (peeled, whole)
2 bunches shallots (washed, root bottoms removed)

Dry seasonings:

2 tablespoons salt
1-1/2 tablespoons black pepper
1-1/2 tablespoons ground cayenne pepper
1-1/2 tablespoons white pepper
3-1/2 tablespoons granulated garlic
2-1/2 tablespoons paprika

Pit:

20 10' lengths of 1/2" or 3/4" EMT conduit
1 spool bailing wire
5'x 6' expanded metal grating
lot hardwood (preferably pecan or hickory)
1 quart cooking oil

Cut an "X" in the pig meat with a sharp filet knife. Stuff one or two toes garlic into each hole, then stuff a shallot into the hole. Cut the shallot at the skin line. Continue stuffing the pig in all the meaty areas until all of the garlic and shallots are used. Don't forget to include the underside of the pig. Mix the seasonings in a stainless steel bowl and dust the pig generously. Pat the seasonings into the pig flesh.

Constructing the Pit:

Dig a 5 foot by 6 foot pit about 12 to 18 inches deep. Cut 3-1/2 foot long pieces from the conduit,. Hammer the cut pieces into the ground, leaving about 14" to 18" sticking out of the ground. Use the bailing wire to lash the longer piece to the stakes to form a grill. Before you put the grating over the pit, wad up newspaper and other kindling and place in the bottom of the pit. Stack 20 to 25 pieces of hardwood in the pit and douse with the cooking oil. Next, place the grating on top of the pit and secure with bailing wire. Run a hose to the pit, this is a great safety measure and might come in handy if the pigs start to fire.

Method

About 15 hours before service, light the pit and allow the wood to burn down to embers. (This will take about 2 hours.) The grill temperature should be very warm but not hot. Place the pig halves skin down on the grill, ensure that no open flame is directly below the meat. Add hot embers to maintain the grill temperature. Turn the once each hour. Concentrate the embers under the shoulders and hams; these areas are thicker and require more heat for the pig to cook evenly. Smoke- roast the pig halves for about 12 hours. When done the bones will literally fall from the meat.

Cochon de Lait (Pronounced: Coo-shon-da-lay)

This Nun I Know

Yvonne, she lived in a cypress shack
In the middle of Bayou Pigeon.
Yvonne, she moved to the town of Dulac
And that's where she got religion.
Not long after she joined a convent,
And she's still a good cook, I admit.
Her recipe for Holy Water
Says… "Boil the HELL out of it!"

(True Story)

St. Landry Shrimp Boulettes

1 pound chopped shrimp
1/8 teaspoon black pepper
1/2 teaspoon salt
1 tablespoon minced onion
2 cloves garlic, minced
1/3 cup minced green onion
1/8 teaspoon ground red pepper
1 egg, well beaten
2 tablespoons milk
1/2 cup dry breadcrumbs
Vegetable oil

In a large bowl, season shrimp with salt and pepper. Add remaining ingredients, except oil; mix well. Form into boulettes (balls), using 1 tablespoon for each ball. Coat boulettes with additional dry bread crumbs. Heat vegetable oil in a heavy skillet, or use a deep fryer. Fry a few at a time 2 minutes each. Remove and drain on paper towels.

Serves 4 to 6.

Fantastique!

Golden Meadow Fried Oysters

2 dozen large raw oysters
1 teaspoon salt
1/2 teaspoon black pepper
1/8 teaspoon cayenne pepper
2 egg yolks
1/2 cup cream
1 cup fine yellow corn meal
1/2 cup flour
1/2 teaspoon garlic powder
1/8 teaspoon salt

Season oysters with 1 teaspoon salt, black pepper, and cayenne. In bowl, beat egg yolks with cream. In another bowl, combine corn meal, flour, garlic powder, and 1/8 teaspoon salt. Mix well.

Dip oysters into egg mixture, then roll in corn meal mixture; coat well. Heat some corn oil in a deep fryer to 375 degrees. Fry oysters about 3 minutes. Drain on paper towel.

Serves 4.

If you're gonna fry oysters, you might as well do it right!

DuPre's Crawfish and Onion Casserole

2 large Vidalia onions, sliced
1 pound crawfish tails
1/2 cup crushed barbecue flavored chips
1 cup Parmesan cheese, grated
1 cup sharp Cheddar cheese, shredded
1 cup Mozzarella cheese, shredded
3 tablespoons butter or margarine
1/2 cup fresh parsley, chopped
1 can cream of mushroom soup
1/2 cup milk
Paprika, to taste
Garlic salt, to taste
Black pepper, to taste

Preheat oven to 350°F. In casserole dish layer one Vidalia onion, 1/4 cup chips, ½ pound crawfish tails, 1/2 cup all cheeses, combined, 1-1/2 tablespoons butter sliced in small pieces, spread out, and 1/4 cup parsley. Repeat layers a second time. Mix soup and milk until mixtures are smooth and creamy. Pour and let settle into casserole over layers. Top with paprika, garlic salt and black pepper. Cook for one hour. May be kept at lower temperature until served. Serve hot with French bread.

Serves 6-8.

A special thanks to Bernadette in Jennings!

Crowley Crawfish Soup

2 cups cooked wild rice (1/2 cup roux)
1 large onion, diced
1/2 green pepper, diced
1-1/2 cup celery, diced
1 small can sliced mushrooms, drained
1/2 cup butter
1 cup flour
8 cups hot chicken broth
1 cup half and half or light cream
2 pounds of crawfish, peeled
Salt, pepper

Sauté' onion, pepper, celery and mushrooms in butter about 3 minutes or until vegetables soften. Sprinkle in the flour, stirring and cooking until flour is mixed but not browned. Slowly add chicken broth, stirring until all are mixed well. Add crawfish and cook about 5 minutes. Add cooked rice and the half and half. Season to taste.

Crowley is the hometown of former Governor Edwin Edwards. I have never met a bad cook from Crowley!

Hushpeoples
(Hushpuppies so hot they hush peoples too!)

1-1/2 cups cornmeal
1 cup flour
3 eggs
1 onion, grated
2-1/2 cups warm milk
1 cup chopped corn
2 teaspoons baking powder
2 teaspoons chopped habanera pepper
1-1/2 cups grated American cheese
2 tablespoons melted butter

Mix the flour and the cornmeal together in a bowl. Beat the eggs
and add to the flour mixture. Add the green onion tops, warm
milk, corn, baking powder and habanera pepper. Stir well. Add
American cheese and the butter. Thoroughly blend ingredients.
Drop into hot oil, a spoonful at a time. Fry until your
Hushpeoples are golden brown in color. Drain on paper towels
and eat.

This one is bound to hush up any big mouth in the family.

Serve them to your least favorite Aunt or the in-law of your choice.

Eat at your own risk!
Wash hands thoroughly after handling habanera peppers!
Do not touch eyes or private parts or any other parts for that matter,
without washing hands with soapy water first.
Don't say I didn't warn ya!

St. Mary Fried Alligator

3 lemons, juiced
1 small bottle Tabasco sauce
1/2 teaspoon salt
1/8 teaspoon black pepper
Water
2 pounds alligator tail meat (Cut into serving sized pieces)
Salt and ground red pepper
Cornmeal and flour, mixed
Corn oil

Combine lemon juice, Tabasco, 1/2 teaspoon salt, black pepper; and enough water to cover the meat. Place meat into large glass bowl and cover with marinade. Marinate in refrigerator 48 hours. Drain well. Season with salt and red pepper to taste. Roll meat in cornmeal and flour mixture. Heat enough oil in pot to deep-fry. Fry the alligator until golden brown.

Serves 6.

You may wonder why you didn't try this sooner!

Easy Street

Needle and thread in Maw Maw's hands
Stitching our Cajun legacies.
A colorific patchwork quilt
Preserving stories and memories.
A handmade broom, a turkey feather fan
Crucifix, candles and rosaries.

A chest of drawers, a string of peppers,
A rag-rug, a small coffee pot.
All we had was all we needed...
Just a little seemed like a lot!
An antique rocker, one GOOD garden...
Simple folk glad for all they got!

Ascension Parish Pork Roast

1 6-pound pork roast
2 cloves garlic, slivered
3 tablespoons slivered onions
2 tablespoons slivered green bell pepper
1 teaspoon salt
1/2 teaspoon black pepper
1/4 teaspoon Tabasco
3 tablespoons corn oil

Make slits in the meat, covering the whole roast. Fill slits with slivered vegetables; press slit to secure firmly. Season meat with salt and peppers. Place oil in Dutch oven; add meat. Roast partially covered in 325-degree oven for about 150 minutes.

Add small amount of water during cooking period. Remove meat to platter. Add 2/3-cup water to drippings; simmer on top of stove until well blended. Serve natural sauce over hot cooked rice.

Serves 10.

In Louisiana our counties are called parishes & there are 64 parishes in the state.
I grew up in Ascension Parish. Gonzales is in Ascension Parish and Gonzales is also "The Jambalaya Capital of the world."

Smuff-a-cated Quail

4 slices bacon
3 tablespoons cooking oil
6 quails
Salt and pepper to taste
4 tablespoons flour
1 large onion, chopped
2 cups chicken broth
2 teaspoons chopped parsley

Fry the bacon until crisp; remove from skillet and set aside. Add oil to skillet. Season the quails with the salt and pepper; brown and set them aside. Add the flour to the skillet; blend well. Add onion; stir-fry until tender.

Return bacon and quails to the skillet. Add remaining ingredients. Bring to a boil; reduce heat; simmer for 30 minutes, or until meat is tender. Serve natural sauce over hot rice.

Serves 6

One of Mrs. Mildred Chauvin's Students got Smothered & Suffocated mixed up and it came out Smuff-a-cated. We thought it was so cute that we decided to use the new word in this recipe.

Calcasieu Rabbit Stew
(Pronounced: Cal-ka-shoo)

large rabbit, dressed
7 tablespoons corn oil
1 large onion, chopped
4 cloves garlic, chopped
1/2 cup tomato paste
4 fresh tomatoes, peeled and chopped
1-1/2 cups water
1 tablespoon Tabasco sauce
Salt and pepper to taste
8 ounces sliced mushrooms
1/2 cup of parsley
1/2 cup green onions

Cut rabbit into serving-size pieces; brown in heated oil; remove. Stir and cook onions and garlic until wilted in same skillet. Add tomato paste; cook 5 minutes.
Add fresh tomatoes and water; stir very well. Cook 20 minutes.
Add rabbit, Tabasco sauce, salt and pepper. Cook for 70 minutes. Add mushrooms, parsley, and green onions right before cooking time is up. Serve over rice.

Serves 6-8.

At a much more rural time Cajuns had to survive on what they gathered from the land around them. The stories of eating possums and other such creatures are more urban myth than fact today.

Iberville Fried Squirrel

1/2 cup vegetable oil
2 squirrels, dressed and cut into bite-size pieces
Salt and black pepper to taste
1 large onion, chopped
Water

Heat oil in a large skillet. Season the meat with salt and pepper; brown well. Add onions; stir and cook until brown. Add 1/2-cup water; stir well. Bring to a boil; reduce heat; simmer for 70 minutes. Check often, adding water as needed. Let water reduce to oil.

Turn meat over once in oil, then remove to serving plate. Add water to drippings to make sauce; simmer 5 minutes. Serve over hot cooked rice.

Serves 5

Will make you scream AIEEE! (And that's a very happy Cajun sound!)

Berwick Beef Bourguignon

3 pounds Cubed Stew Beef
1-1/2 cups Brandy
2-1/2 cups Red Wine
1/2 cup Butter
1/2 pound Whole Mushrooms
1/2 pound Pearl Onions
4 tablespoons Tomato Paste
2 Cloves Chopped Garlic
1 Bay Leaf
1/2 tsp Thyme
One 10.5 ounce Can Beef Stock
1/4 cup Flour

Marinate beef in 1/3 of brandy and red wine for at least 1 hour. Turn occasionally. In large heavy skillet heat half the butter until foamy. Mix together flour with salt and pepper to taste.

Roll beef cubes in flour, place in hot butter and brown, removing cubes as they are done. In separate skillet, heat remaining butter; add onions; stir, cover and simmer over low heat 2 min. Add mushrooms, turn up heat and sauté 3 minutes. Remove from heat; add tomato paste, garlic and 1 tablespoon flour. Mix until smooth. Add remaining brandy, red wine, beef stock, bay leaf, thyme, salt / pepper to taste. boil, reduce heat. Simmer 15 minutes. Add beef and simmer 1-1/2 hours.

Serves 6.

Heritage

"Jambalaya, Crawfish Pie, Filé Gumbo…"
Hank Williams wrote a song about us long ago.
And through the years it seems the world has come to know,
The happiness of every *Thibodeaux & Fontenot.
"Pick guitar, fill fruit jar" Oh, It's a song that we love so…
"Jambalaya, Crawfish Pie, Filé Gumbo."

(* Pronounced: Tib-a-doe & Fon-ta-no)

Coush Coush

2 cups cornmeal
1/2 teaspoon salt
1 1/2 cups boiling water
2 teaspoons baking powder
3 eggs, beaten
1 teaspoon shortening

Stir cornmeal and salt into water. Cool and add baking powder and eggs. Preheat skillet with shortening and pour in mixture. Cook over medium heat for five minutes. Serve immediately in cereal bowls with cold milk - like eating cornbread and milk.

This is a very old and basic Cajun dish.

Peter Piper's (ASS KICKING) Party Pepper Pops
Another Eat At Your OWN Risk Recipe!

6 (12-ounce) cans hot jalapeno peppers 1 pound Velveeta (coarsely grated) 1 tablespoon habanera pepper, finely chopped

Drain and remove stems from peppers. (All seeds must be removed from peppers.) Mix chopped habanera with cheese and stuff into jalapenos.

6 (6-ounce) cans crabmeat
2 cups mayonnaise
4 (7-1/2 ounce) cartons Egg Beaters (Vegetable Omelet Mix)
4 tablespoons onion, minced
2 tablespoons Italian seasoning
2 tablespoons All That Jazz Cajun & Creole Blast
2 (15-ounce) boxes Italian bread crumbs

Combine all remaining ingredients and mix together well.
Pat mixture into small patties 1/4 inch thick.
Patties must be large enough to wrap around the stuffed pepper.
Mixture should seal off entire surface of pepper.
Deep fry for 5 minutes in hot oil.
Should be browned.
Makes 42

Guaranteed to fix clogged sinuses & constipation too!

These are best when chased with Abita Purple Haze (Raspberry Wheat Beer)
See Abita.com

All That Jazz
Cajun & Creole Blast

3 Teaspoons of salt
1/4 cup of onion powder
1/4 cup of garlic powder
2 tablespoons of paprika
1 tablespoon of cayenne pepper
1 tablespoon of black pepper
1-1/2 teaspoons of chili powder
1-1/2 teaspoons of celery seed
1/2 teaspoon nutmeg
1 teaspoon lemon pepper

Combine the various ingredients (listed above)
into a bowl and stir until blended well.
The amount of cayenne may be decreased or increased
for a milder or hotter seasoning preference. Makes 1 cup.

*Note: "All That Jazz: Cajun & Creole Blast," is the copyrighted
creation of Saint–Pierre Enterprises and WordBlossoms.com.*

Let's Do It In The Kitchen
(Crawfish Boil From Scratch)

15 pounds live crawfish
2 boxes of salt
1 teaspoon crushed red pepper
4 bay leaves, crumbled
1 tablespoon allspice
3 tablespoons mustard seed
1 teaspoon whole cloves
2 tablespoons whole coriander
1/4 teaspoon black pepper
2 teaspoons Tabasco
1 tablespoon paprika

Put crawfish in a tub of salt and water. Let them sit until they calm down. Rinse with clean water. This is called purging the crawfish.

In an extra-large pot, bring 5 quarts of water to a full rolling boil. Make a bag out of cheesecloth; put all the seasonings in the bag; tie. Place the bag in the boiling water.
Drop a few pounds of crawfish at a time into full boiling water. Cover pot. Return water to a full boil. Cook about 5 minutes.

Remove from water. Serve on a large platter.

Let everyone peel their own.

Serves 6.

Crawfish boils are very popular social get-togethers in South Louisiana. (A lot like cookouts or barbeques elsewhere)

If you'd like to have your own Crawfish Boil, no matter where you are in the United States, check out OnTheSpot.com, they ship everything you need for a small group or a large party right to your own front door!

A Microwave Roux By Lazy Lou

1 cup flour
1 cup oil
1 cup chopped onions
1/2 cup chopped celery
1/4 cup chopped bell pepper
3 cloves garlic, minced
1/4 cup chopped parsley

Combine flour and oil in 2 quart bowl. Microwave on high for 8 to 9 minutes. stir at 2 Minutes. Stir again at 1 minute. Stir again at end of cooking. Add remaining ingredients and microwave on high for 5 minutes. Stir at 3 minutes and at end of cooking time. Veggies should be soft. Pour oil off top. This roux freezes well.

Freeze extra for future use.

Lou is just too lazy to make a roux right, but I must say I was surprised by how well this method works!

Hotter Than Hell Sabbath Dip
(From a Drag Queen in New Orleans who Claims to be The
Original Creole Lady Marmalade)

1/2 *far out* cup chopped purple Creole onion
1/2 *get-down* cup chopped celery
2 *outa-site* tablespoons habanera pepper, chopped finely
2-1/2 *tripping* tablespoons of real butter
1 *funky* (3-ounce) can sliced mushrooms, drained
1 *groovy* (10-ounce) package frozen chopped turnip greens
1/4 *zesty teaspoon* grated lemon rind
1/4 *zippy teaspoon* grated lime rind
1 *skinny-pinch* of paprika
1 *penny-pinch* of celery seed
1 *way-cool* (10-ounce) can cream of mushroom soup
1 *happening* (6-ounce) package garlic cheese spread
1-1/2 *hip* teaspoons Worcestershire sauce
7 *magical* drops of Louisiana Hot Sauce
1 *tantalizing* teaspoon of All
That Jazz Cajun & Creole Blast

*Sauté that celery and them Creole onions in y'all's butter until they are
soft. Stir in those mushrooms and put them to the side for now, babies.
Then put those turnip greens, along with the lemon and lime rind and
the chopped jalapeno pepper in the bowl of y'all's food processor, and
process it until it is some kind of smooth and puréed. In the top of a
double boiler, combine y'all's sautéed vegetables, puréed turnip greens,
soup, cheese, Worcestershire, Louisiana Hot Sauce, paprika, celery seed
and All That Jazz Cajun & Creole Blast, stirring it up till all y'all's*

ingredients are married real good, and not just shacked up and livin in sin. Now make shore it's heated real good girlfriend. Then you gonna wanna serve it up hot with some tia chips or even better with some of Mr. St. Pierre's Coonass Cornbread, Honey!

I'll promise y'all one fricken thing...this "Some Like It Hot" Creole dip will burn more on the end it comes out of than it does on the end it goes into, but I think you can handle it Miss Thang! I hope y'all like S & M coz you shore gonna have to be into pain to appreciate the "Hurt So Good" pleasure of this lovely party appetizer!

Oh and by the way...Male or female y'all have absolutely got to make this dip in the buff wearing high heel shoes! You're on your own now! If y'all knew how busy I stay y'all wouldn't be bothering me for a damn recipe!

Oysters in Pig's Clothing

1 dozen fresh, shucked oysters (in a jar)
1/4 cup of oyster liquid (from jar)
1 bay leaf
1 teaspoons Worcestershire sauce
4 slices (1/2 ounce each) lean,
Raw bacon
1/2 cup unbleached white flour
(in a small bowl)
2 eggs (beaten in a small Bowl)
1 cup Bread crumbs
2 cups Oil (for frying)
12 toothpicks (for wrapping Bacon)

In a 1 quart saucepan, on a medium flame, poach oysters in oyster liquor with bay leaf and Worcestershire (about 2 minutes, until the edges of the oysters curl). Remove oysters from liquor and set aside. Discard liquor.

Cut bacon strips in thirds. Wrap each oyster with bacon and fasten with a toothpick. Roll in flour, dip in eggs, and then roll in breadcrumbs.

Heat oil in a 9-inch skillet. When oil smokes, reduce heat and fry oysters for 5 minutes. Drain on paper bag and serve immediately.

Yields 12 oysters.

Gold Untold

The legendary pirate Jean Lafitte,
Had supposedly hidden beaucoups of gold.
Tons upon tons of real buried treasure,
With gold coins and trinkets and wealth untold.

Oh, people have searched for many a year.
They dream of finding that great secret spot.
Like the gold they say is at rainbow's end;
Someone might find it, but probably not.

Still, in Louisiana hopes run high.
Though their hopes and dreams may just go KAPUT!
One day, who knows? Some Cajun could shout out...
"Low and behold the gold of Jean LaFOOT!"

Jean Lafitte: A Louisiana Legend!

History-Mystery

Marie LaVeau, as you may well know,
Was known as the Voodoo Queen.
Her skin they say, was like Café Au Lait,
Her eyes were a magical green.

Marie she was misunderstood,
Though many considered her evil.
The spells she cast were mostly good,
Soothing pains or calming upheaval.

Marie knew voodoo like so few do,
In the Big Easy long ago.
One of history's greatest mysteries
Is the legendary Marie LaVeau.

Marie LaVeau's Grave in New Orleans is probably the most
visited gravesite in Louisiana.

Children Beware

Beware, the mean Marsh Monster!
Behave before it's too late!
You need not ever worry,
If you clean your room and clean your plate!

He creeps in from the dark swamp,
Silent and undetected.
They say he's bound to show up
Just when you least expect it.

Be wise; do not tell lies!
Be good and always be true!
Because that hungry werewolf
Is most likely watching you!

Children beware, or be eaten
By that crazy old Loup Garou!

Loup Garou (Loo garoo)- A mythical creature who legend says
lurks in the South Louisiana Swamps and turns from a man to a
wolf at twilight; A Cajun Werewolf.

Sonnier's Pain Perdu
(French Toast) Sonnier: Pronounced "Saun-yea."

1 loaf (18-20 inches) dry French bread
3 eggs
1/2 cup milk
3 tablespoons butter
Confectioner's sugar
Nutmeg

Carefully slice bread into 3/4 inch slices. Mix eggs and milk in a shallow, flat dish. Do not beat until frothy.

Dip bread slices and turn to coat both sides. Set aside on plate for 5 minutes while melting 1-tablespoon butter in skillet.

Heat to medium high and fry as many slices as will cover the skillet bottom. Turn when light brown, adding butter if necessary. Move the slices while cooking and adjust heat in order to brown evenly. Continue until all bread is fried.
Serve hot with sprinkled nutmeg and sifted confectioners sugar.

Serves 4-6.

I grew up thinking that everyone ate Pain Perdu for breakfast. (I guess everyone wasn't as lucky as me!)
Personally I love to dip mine in "STEEN'S CANE SYRUP."
About STEEN'S...

Four generations of the Steen family have produced this syrup, which is still sold in an old-fashioned, bright yellow can that any Louisiana native would know instantly. To make the "100% Pure & Natural" syrup, cane sugar is ground, the juice extracted, and the resultant mixture simmered in large open kettles until it reaches the right clarity and consistency. The process is done according to the original recipe, perfected by Charlie Steen in 1910 in Abbeville, Louisiana. "Great when poured over hot biscuits too!"

You may order online at www.Steensyrup.com

Patterson Bread Pudding

16 slices day old bread torn into 1" pieces
1-1/2 cups sugar
1/2 cup Steen's Cane Syrup
4 eggs
2 teaspoons cinnamon
1/2 teaspoon salt
2 tablespoons vanilla extract
3/4 cup apple sauce
2 cups coarsely chopped pecans
1 cup golden raisins
3/4 cup margarine or butter, melted
3 cups milk

In a large bowl, combine bread sugar and syrup. Set aside.

In another bowl, beat milk, cinnamon, salt and vanilla until foamy. Pour over bread and sugar. Mix well. Cover and refrigerate 2 hours.

Stir in remaining ingredients except cream. Pour into a greased 13"x9"x2" baking pan.
Bake at 350 degrees for 50 minutes or until firm. Cut into squares. Serve warm or cold with whipped cream.

From Mrs. Richard (Ree-shard)

Bourgeois Bread Pudding
(Bourgeois pronounced: Bouge-wah)

4 cups bread cubes
1/4 teaspoon salt
2 cups milk
2 eggs, beaten
1/2 cup Steen's Cane Syrup
1/2 cup raisins
1/4 cup butter
Rum Sauce:
1 stick butter
2 tablespoons flour
2 teaspoon vanilla
1/4 teaspoon butter flavoring
1 cup water
3/4 cup sugar
2 teaspoons rum flavoring

Spread bread cubes evenly in 8" round dish. Sprinkle evenly with brown sugar and salt, then raisins. Measure milk in quart measuring cup. Add butter. Microwave at high for 4 minutes, until butter is melted and milk is warm.

Rapidly stir in eggs with a fork and mix well. Pour over bread cubes in dish. Microwave on medium high 9 to 12 minutes, rotating dish one-half turn after 6 minutes. When cooked, center may still be slightly soft but it will set up as pudding cools.

Sauce:

In saucepan, bring butter and water to boil. Add premixed flour
and sugar. Add remaining ingredients and cook until bubble.
Remove from heat and serve hot over pudding.

Serves 6

This recipe could easily be subtitled Instant SINsation.

New Iberia Praline Cake

2 cups pecans, coarsely chopped
1 cup light brown sugar, packed
5 tablespoons Steen's Cane Syrup
1-1/4 sticks margarine, melted
1 box butter pecan cake mix
1-1/4 cups water
1/3 cup vegetable oil
3 eggs

Preheat oven to 325 degrees.

Mix pecans, brown sugar, syrup and margarine in a bowl. Generously spray pan with cooking spray. Spread the mixture evenly in the bottom of the pan. Prepare cake mix as directed on package. Pour batter slowly over mixture in pan.

Bake until cake springs back when touched lightly in center. Bake about 45 minutes to an hour.

When done, immediately invert pan onto a heat-proof tray or covered board. Leave pan over cake for 5 minutes. Remove pan. Can be served with ice cream or whipped topping.

Ladies: If you're out to catch yourself a man, make him one of these cakes and he'll be ALL YOURS!

Cajun Carrot Cake

4 eggs, beaten
2 cups sugar
1-1/2 cups oil
2 cups flour
1 pound carrots, grated
1 teaspoon cinnamon
1 teaspoon salt
1 teaspoon baking soda
1 cup pecans, chopped
One 8-ounce package cream cheese
4 teaspoons butter, melted
1 pound powdered sugar
1 teaspoon vanilla
1/2 cup pecans, chopped
1 teaspoon Tabasco

Preheat oven to 350°F. Cream eggs and sugar together. Mix in oil, flour, carrots, cinnamon, Tabasco, salt and baking soda. Blend well, then mix in chopped pecans.

Bake. While cake is cooling, make frosting by blending cream cheese, melted butter, powdered sugar, vanilla and chopped pecans. Frost cake after it is fully cooled.

Serves 10.

Delightfully Different!

The Blessing of the Fleet

Way down to Morgan City,
That's where you have to go.
Where some folks make a living
In the Gulf of Mexico.

The fishermen ask blessings,
With hopes for a bountiful yield.
Prayers for each- other's safety,
And a fertile fishing field...

"As we go forth, Lord guide us
Through the storms and through the heat.
We know you're right beside us,
Grant your blessings to our fleet."

Big Easy Bananas Foster

2 tablespoons butter
3 tablespoons brown sugar
2 large bananas, sliced
3 tablespoons banana liqueur
3 cups rum
Juice of 1 orange
Juice of 1/2 lemon
Vanilla ice cream

Heat butter in frying pan over medium heat. When melted, add sugar and mix well. Cook until golden brown. Add sliced bananas and mix well; cook 1 minute.

Add fruit juices, mix, and continue cooking 1 minute. Add liqueur and rum. Flambé. Mix well and serve over vanilla ice cream.

Serves 4.

A Magnificent New Orleans' Dessert!

Pauline's Pralines

2 cups of white sugar
1 cup of buttermilk
1 teaspoon of baking soda
2 cups of pecan halves
1 teaspoon of pure vanilla extract

Combine sugar, buttermilk, and baking soda in a heavy 5 quart pot. With a wooden or plastic spoon, stir this mixture constantly on high just until it begins to boil. Reduce the heat to medium and continue to stir constantly.

The mixture will rise and then fall back down. Continue to stir constantly until the mixture turns light brown and reaches a soft-ball stage approximately 15 to 20 minutes.
(Drop a small amount of mixture into a bowl of water to test for soft ball stage.
A candy thermometer can also he used to test for the soft ball stage of 234°F.)

Remove the pot from the heat after the mixture reaches the soft-ball stage. Add the pecans and vanilla. Stir the mixture until it starts to lose its gloss. At this point, quickly spoon out the mixture onto aluminum foil to your desired size. Let the pralines cool and then remove them from the foil.

Serves 2 dozen.

Guaranteed to fix your sweet-tooth!

Bordelonville Praline Cookies

3/4 cup butter
1-1/2 cups brown sugar, packed
1 egg
1 teaspoon vanilla
1-1/2 cups sifted all-purpose flour
1 cup chopped pecans

Cream butter until smooth. Add sugar and egg. Beat until smooth and fluffy. Add vanilla. Sift in flour; blend thoroughly. Stir in pecans. Shape into balls, using 1 level tablespoon of dough for each.

On a buttered baking sheet, flatten balls to 1/8-inch thickness, spacing 1-inch apart. Bake in preheated 375-degree oven for 12 minutes. Cool.

Makes 3 dozen.

From Mrs. Robert (Row-Bear) in St. Amant, Louisiana.

Thanks but No Thanks

We thank you for the good health,
For the crops of berries and grain.
Thank you for the gifts you send,
EXCEPT for that old HURRICANE!

Batiste Blackberry Cobbler

1 cup flour
3 teaspoons baking powder
1 cup sugar
1/8 teaspoon salt
1 cup evaporated milk
2 teaspoons vanilla
1 tablespoon cornstarch
3/4 cup sugar
1/2 cup hot water
1 tablespoon fresh lemon juice
3 cups fresh blackberries
2 tablespoons butter

Mix together flour, baking powder, 1 cup sugar and salt; blend well. Stir in milk and vanilla. Pour mixture into greased 7x11-inch glass baking dish. Mix together cornstarch and 3/4 cup sugar. Add hot water; stir well. Add lemon juice and blackberries; mix well. Slowly pour into the center of batter. Dot with butter. Bake in 350-degree oven for 35 minutes. Serve warm with vanilla ice cream.

Serves 8.

From the purple and gold iris lady in Lake Martin.

Louisiana Pecan Pie

5 tablespoons butter
3/4 cup sugar
3 eggs, slightly beaten
3/4 cup Steen's Pure Cane syrup
1/4 teaspoon salt
1-1/2 teaspoons vanilla
3/4 cup coarsely chopped pecans
1/2 cup flaked coconut
Pecan halves for top
1 9-inch unbaked pie crust

Cream butter and sugar; beat until light and fluffy. Add eggs, syrup, salt, vanilla, chopped pecans, and coconut. Mix well. Pour into pie crust. Top with pecan halves. Bake in preheated 400-degree oven for 10 minutes. Reduce heat to 350-degrees; bake about 40 minutes. Serve with vanilla ice cream. Makes 1 pie.

Laissez les bon temps roulez! (Let the good times roll!)

Papa Noel

Build the bonfires on the levee,
Along the Mississippi River.
The air is cold the logs are heavy,
Build the bonfires, shiver-shiver.

I can hear the locust humming,
Build the bonfires, build them well.
That Cajun Santa is coming,
We welcome our Papa Noel.

Papa Noel: Cajun Santa Clause who rides a sleigh-boat pulled
by alligators down the Mississippi River to bring presents
to the Cajuns on Christmas Eve.

Cajun Christmas Egg Nog

6 quarts egg nog
1-1/2 gallons milk
4 half-gallons vanilla ice cream
3 fifths bourbon
1 teaspoon Tabasco
Ground nutmeg

In large container, mix together the egg nog and milk. Add large scoops of ice cream.
Blend in the whiskey and Tabasco. Sprinkle with nutmeg.

Makes 3 gallons.

Cajun Rap
(By a plain white rapper)

In Lafayette and Thibodaux
They sure know how to Fais-do-do
From Baton Rouge to Monroe
We have it good, hey, don't you know.
Venice, Eunice, Anacoco
Church Point, New Roads and Lebeau
Turkey Creek and Shreveport too
From Plain Dealing to Big Mamou
From Gonzales to Shongaloo.
Pecan Island is waiting for you.
Ville Platte, Jennings and Tallulah
From the town of Ruston to Bayou Goula.
Leesville, Marksville, Ponchatoula
Winnfield, Carville, Cocodrie,
Coushatta, Minden, Gramercy.
In Bogalusa or Zachary
Slidell, Oakdale, Grand Bayou
Opelousas and Mansfield too.
From Natchitoches to Morgan City
St. Francisville is so pretty
Belle Rose, Belle Chasse, Carencro
Houma, Hammond, Westwego.
Near and far and high and low
French Settlement and Grand Coteau
Covingington, St. Martinville,
Kentwood, Rayne and Forest Hill
Cottonport and Abbeville

De Ridder, Scott and Springhill.
From Lake Charles to Pierre Part
Sweet Louisiana is in my heart.
Cut Off, Zwolle, Calcasieu
Lake Providence, Golden Meadow too.
New Orleans is waiting for you.
Franklin, Farmerville, Bastrop, wow!
Greenwood, Greensburg, let's go now.
From Alexandria to Grand Isle
We have lagniappe, we have style.
You can have Paris and you can keep Rome.
Louisiana is my home sweet home.

Lagniappe: (Lan-Yap) An extra-unexpected gift or benefit.

Le bon seigneur vous bénira! (The good Lord will bless you!)

About the Author

Todd-Michael St. Pierre was born in New Orleans, Louisiana, and currently lives in Baton Rouge. He is a writer and recipe developer for America's top cooking magazines. He is also the author of *The Louisiana State Bird Beauty Pageant,* a picture book for children.

Todd-Michael is currently working on a new cookbook entitled *Magical Mardi Gras Cuisine* and a new children's book *The Cajun Mouse & The Creole Mouse.*

1-931600-33-3